Maya's Tale

Maya's Tale

One dachshund's journey from puppy mill to pampered princess

Yvonne Haldeman Moyer

The interior of this book was rendered primarily in the Georgia font. The cover was adapted from *Redstripe and Other Dachshund Tales,* originally designed by Charles King (CKMM.com) as a work for hire, Copyright © 2003 by Unlimited Publishing LLC. The interior and/or cover designs of this book incorporate one or more fonts specifically licensed by and customized for the exclusive use of Unlimited Publishing LLC, which may not be reproduced elsewhere in any form without written permission from the publisher.

First Edition
ISBN:9781475085198
PENDING

This fine book and many others are available at:
http://www.unlimitedpublishing.com

Unlimited Publishing LLC is a proud member of the Independent Book Publishers Association (IBPA-online.org), serving thousands of publishers across North America and around the world since 1983.

Preface

IN FEBRUARY of 2000, I had gone for a girl's day out shopping with my girlfriend Bonnie. On a whim, we went into a Petland store, just to "look" at the puppies. We slowly browsed down the aisle of puppy cages, when there, in a cage all by himself, was a tiny black and tan Miniature Dachshund puppy curled up in a tight little ball. My mind immediately flashed back to my Pappy and his dachshund Fritz, who were an inseparable pair. Those emotional memories, prompted a desire to hold this little pup too strong to ignore, and I soon found myself waiting in a small cubicle in the center of the store until an employee brought the puppy from his cage to the "visiting area." He was adorable, playful, affectionate, and of course, I fell in love with him right then and there. After finding out the cost of this pup was $700.00, my adoration faded a bit and Bonnie and I both exited the store empty handed, yet wishing to be taking a puppy home with us. We made it to the car, where we sat and debated the Shih Tzu she had seen. We also discussed the dachshund I had my eye on. I was already feeling an attachment to the little guy. Bonnie kept her resolve. I did not. Thirty minutes later, we were back in the car. This time I was holding a 12 week old wiener dog pup.

On the way back to Bonnie's house, I was thrilled to have this little guy in my lap, anxious to see my son's reaction to this unexpected addition to our family and yet still stunned that I had paid so much money on an impulse. When we arrived at the house, I put the pup inside my coat, out of sight. Naturally, upon entering the door, my son's first question was, "Mom, did you bring me anything?" As I was sitting down, and before I could answer his question, that little pup stuck his head up and out of my coat, just as if he had been given his entrance cue. We all laughed, knowing then that this pup was going to be a real ham. I set him on the floor and he proceeded to excitedly race around the coffee table seven or eight times, just as fast as his stubby legs could go, and this proved to be the inspiration for his name, "Zippy."

Zippy fit into our home very quickly and had no problem bonding with my son and our two existing house cats, Cricket and Kadydid. A few days after joining our family, Zippy was taken to the Petland approved veterinarian for his health check and to activate his health warranty. I was told that he was a nice looking and healthy pup and to immediately wean him off the brand of puppy food that the pet store had sent home with him. The vet reported this brand of food was known to cause gastro-intestinal upset quite frequently. Now having activated his warranty, I did change his food and also took him to the veterinarian that I had been using for several years and trusted. He also declared him to be a nice looking, healthy pup, who would probably not be over ten pounds when fully grown. Feeling confident that he was in good health and was settling in to our home well, I now filled out his AKC registration papers and sent them in, with his official name listed as, "Wayne's Zippity Doo Dah."

We began the housetraining process by "crate training" quickly realizing that Zippy did not like to be left alone and absolutely hated, going into his crate. He proved to be difficult to housebreak. After many accidents, a lot of frustration, and many frigid mornings, standing outside, waiting for him to do his business, we accomplished our goal. Having reached this accomplishment, I felt we could try leaving him out of the crate, which was such a nightmare to both of us; I began by using a baby gate to confine him to small rooms at first. Somehow, he always managed to get past the gate, leave it standing, and then shred any paper or cloth he could find. A dog trainer was called to provide assistance and many different techniques were attempted, all to no avail. Those first six months were surely trying at times and yet there was a lot of laughter and joy while we learned his personality and watched him learn and experience new things.

He was definitely stubborn, but also bold, fearless, and curious. He loved watermelon and would eat a slice just like his people did, starting at the top, and working from side to side until down to the rind. I also discovered that first summer, that he loved strawberries. I had a small row of them in my garden, watched them bud, form berries, grow larger and start to turn pink. Just before they were ripe enough to pick, they would disappear. Darn birds, was my first thought. Then one evening, I happened to glance out the window, noticing Zippy over by the strawberry patch. I continued to observe as he ever so delicately took a strawberry in his mouth, gently pulled it from the plant and proceeded to eat it before moving up the row to the next plant. I had caught the real culprit red pawed, so to speak. A small piece of border fencing solved that problem, and we did get a handful of berries that summer, but Zippy definitely got the majority of them.

By now, Zippy and the older cat Cricket, had become best buddies, often curling up to sleep side by side. Zippy taught both cats how to race laps around the household furniture. Cricket, especially enjoyed this game and would engage in the activity anytime Zip was ready to run. Kady, on the other hand, was not inclined to demean herself this way often. When she did, the three of them racing and cavorting from room to room, sounded like a herd of elephants had been let loose to romp about the house.

Later that year, one of the TV news programs aired a piece on pet stores and how they acquired puppies from puppy farms. The story focused on the cruel conditions of these farms, and the deceptive practices of the pet stores to appeal to prospective buyers. As I watched this program, lo and behold, Petland was specifically mentioned in this piece. I knew from Zippy's registration papers that he had come to a West Virginia pet store from a Missouri breeder. I immediately began to suspect that he may have been a victim of the exact process described in the program. A phone call to the Petland store yielded assurances from the manager that their store did not participate in the practices described in the news program piece. An internet search gave me no specific information on that particular breeder. I was disturbed by the realization of how these puppies were coming into our hearts and homes under deceptive circumstances and yet knew that I would probably never know for certain Zippy's early life. The only thing I felt I could do now, was to make sure Zippy lived a good life and that I never purchased another pet from a pet store again.

When Zippy was a year and a half old, we moved to a new town. Everybody adjusted well and many new activities and opportunities were available.

We joined a dog agility club, where Zippy learned to run an agility course and became a certified Therapy Dog. We had a larger house for all 3 animals to run laps in, and it was pretty much a daily activity for Cricket and Zippy to run around the dining room table. First Zippy chasing Cricket, then they would abruptly change direction and Cricket would chase Zippy. One day, in particular, a contractor was in the house when this activity began. The amazement was clearly visible on his face as he told me, "You need to tape that and send it in to that funny video show." I never did tape that activity, but I did tape Zippy in the car at the carwash. I still don't know for sure if he loves the carwash or hates it, but his reaction is pretty dramatic. The water jets appear to be his arch enemy as he frantically runs across the back seat from window to window, barking and jumping at the water. When the water is going across the back window, he tries to jump up to it, he looks like a black and tan Mexican Jumping Bean. I have never heard from that show, but, that's okay. Sometimes we go to the carwash, just as a treat for Zippy.

The neighborhood children have figured out that if they run up and down along the fence line, Zippy will race them endlessly. Usually Zippy wins, even when the kids try to get a head start or to sneak up on him. The backyard is Zip's domain and he patrols and defends it with all of his might. No other dog is allowed near his yard without hearing his vocal protest and any unknown person walking by will also be met with this same declaration. There are a couple of adult male neighbors that Zip is normally very friendly with when out of his yard; yet when they are near "his" backyard, are met with his possessive defense display. These men find it amusing to reach over the fence toward Zip, while he is barking as fiercely as his small frame allows. One might think they would know better and that this is asking for trouble. Not with Zip, he will turn his head just enough that the intruding hand is right beside his muzzle, while he continues to bark. If the hand is moved, he adjusts his head to maintain that position, never touching the hand, but still barking his protest. Thankfully, the men do grow bored with this game and cease invading Zip's turf.

Cricket has begun to noticeably slow down. She is now sixteen years old, and Kadydid is nine. They both began to have health issues. Cricket started having seizures and losing weight dramatically. It was frightening for all of us to see her having a seizure and it also appeared to be painful for her. After every seizure, she would slowly walk the perimeter of every room in the house, as if she had never been there before. Our vet could not find anything physically wrong with her, other than her advanced age. He prescribed an anti-seizure medication. The medication decreased the severity of the seizures, but she continued to lose weight over the next six months.

One afternoon, while resting on the couch with Cricket furled up beside me, she looked at me in a way she never had before; I knew she was suffering. I looked at her, and saw that she had truly lost half of her body weight and was dull and lethargic as well. It was coming to her time to go. I loved her too much to keep her suffering and in pain for my own selfish desires. I called the vet the next day and scheduled an appointment for the following day. I spent that day holding her and trying to feed her shrimp that she would not eat. I cried profusely most of that day. After taking my son to school the following day, I thought I was prepared and drove Cricket to the vet for the last time. My heart was breaking. I was not prepared and began crying again before I even got there. She had been through so much with me, a gift from an ex-boyfriend, who found her at the animal shelter, she was with me through a marriage, the birth of my only child, a divorce, the building of my new life and the diagnosis of Muscular Dystrophy for my son. I walked into the vet's office a mess. The staff there assured me this was the right decision and they treated both Cricket and me with love and respect. One staff member took Cricket into the procedure area, while another walked me out to my car for privacy. They then brought Cricket's body out to me, carefully wrapped in a blanket and tucked into a cardboard pet coffin. We sat in the parking lot until I was ready to drive back home. After school was over, we buried

Cricket in the front flower bed. Roses had always been her favorite flower. Anytime I had cut roses in the house, she would chew on them. She never actually ate them, but I would find tooth marks on the petals. She never bothered with any other type of plant or flower. We appropriately planted a red rose bush by her grave, our memorial to her.

While we were dealing with the beginning of Cricket's seizure disorder, Kadydid began to have problems with her teeth. It turned out that she had a condition where her body was actually rejecting her teeth. It was recommended that the affected teeth be removed. We had this done and she was better for a good while. Then, after Cricket was gone, Kady became mean and isolated herself in Wayne's bedroom. She would hiss and growl at anyone who entered the room and eventually she began to attempt biting Wayne when he went to bed. A consultation with the vet revealed that this could continue until all her teeth would have to be removed and that left untreated could lead to massive infection and be fatal. So, just a few months after Cricket was put down, I decided I could not have an animal in the home that could potentially harm my son, nor could I let Kady continue to suffer with the obvious pain and misery she was experiencing. Kady was also put down, but at Wayne's request, her body was not brought home. He had picked her out as a kitten. She was always his cat and he did not want to see her "empty body." He wanted to remember her happy and silly, like she was before she got sick. A pink rose bush joined the red one in the front flower bed, Kady's memorial.

Now, for the first time since we brought Zippy home, he was the only pet in the house. Soon it became obvious he did not like being the sole pet. He started acting moody and nervous, hated being left alone and was not eating as well as he had in the past, often refusing to eat for two or three days at a time. One day in particular, while I was working in the flower beds, he escaped from our yard, went to the neighbor's house and began trying to play with her outside cats. Her German Shepherd saw him from inside the house, forced her way out the door, charged Zippy and rolled him over once in the middle of the street. Zippy escaped her grasp and ran home as fast as his little legs would carry him. He did manage to out run the shepherd to the safety of his porch. The neighbor and I both had seen the situation unfolding but it all happened faster than either of us could react. Zippy vaulted himself up the three steps to the front porch, I positioned myself between him and the shepherd, armed myself with a broom, causing the shepherd to pause just long enough for her owner, who was only five or six steps behind, to gain control of her dog, restrain her and safely return her to their house. Trembling from the experience, I picked Zippy up and found that the inside of his lip was bleeding and that he was trembling far more than I was. The neighbor then came across the street to check if we were both alright. She confirmed, that her dog did indeed have all of her shots up to date and that she had seen Zippy outside, playing with the cats, like he always did when I took him for a walk. As she was opening her door, the shepherd pushed past her and jumped Zip before he even saw her coming. Another look at Zippy's lip showed the bleeding had stopped and it was just a slight scratch. He had no trouble recovering physically.

After that experience, Zippy's behavior changed even more. He became fearful of any dog bigger than him, which at exactly ten pounds, is almost every dog we would encounter. I realized how vulnerable he was to other dogs, and I feel that we began to feed each other's fears. The vet, and our agility trainer, helped me utilize some techniques that enabled me to let go of my fear and to build Zippy's confidence back up. Slowly, we improved together and were able to enjoy our walks and outings again. After about a year, I began to see that he was lonely. Our home was feeling empty. We had plenty of room and love for another pet.

CHAPTER 1

IT HAD BEEN five years since there had been a new pet in our home, and after some difficult times, we were ready to open our hearts again. There had been several opportunities to bring a new kitten into our lives, but, I just couldn't do it. They just weren't Cricket or Kady. So, my focus was on another dog. Zippy needed a buddy, somebody who would enjoy the same things he did, crawling under anything he could fit under (the dirtier the space the better), catching birds in the backyard (yes, he thought he was a bird dog), going for walks, running circles around the furniture, tearing the stuffing and squeakers out of toys, curling up under a blanket, going to the carwash, running agility, visiting nursing homes and racing along the fence line. I decided on another dachshund, and thought that a female would be an easier adjustment for Zippy to accept. I began looking online at dachshund rescue sites and spotted a longhaired miniature dachshund female that was only a year old. She was gorgeous, black and tan, with a long silky coat and soft brown eyes that just melted your heart.

Further inquiries revealed that she was already chosen to be adopted. I was disappointed but, now knew what our next addition would be; I just had to find the right one. I left word with our local shelters and vet offices, watched the rescue sites and newspaper ads, asked around and searched on line for a dachshund breeder. I absolutely would not consider a pet store; the news report on Petland and other pet stores was not forgotten. This went on for several months with no luck for what I had my heart set on; a long-haired, female, black and tan miniature dachshund.

Out of the blue, on a Saturday morning in November, I received a phone call from a lady who told me she had what I was looking for. Since it was early in the morning over the Thanksgiving holiday, I was disoriented not knowing what she was talking about. As she began to explain that a fellow breeder, had contacted her with information that I was looking for a specific type of dog to adopt, my wits returned in time to understand that she had a litter of long-haired miniature dachshund pups that were black and tan and included two females. My heart started to race with excitement over finally having a viable lead, but I contained my excitement and brought forth my logical side and began to ask, all of the questions I had learned to be important when talking to a breeder. As our conversation continued, I learned that the pups were twelve weeks old, the parents were both on the premises and owned by the breeder. She had been breeding dachshunds and three other small breeds of dogs, for over 30 years. She had references from her veterinarian and previous customers. The puppies had been given their shots and came with a health guarantee that required an exam, by my own veterinarian, within 48 hours after purchase. The breeder then began to ask questions about our household, our existing pets, their roles and activities in the home and who our veterinarian was. She reported knowing our vet, and had sold puppies to some of his clients in the past. I felt good enough, after our exchange, to ask for directions to come and see the puppies and possibly purchase one. The breeder then told me that she was leaving the next afternoon for an out of state wedding, and that she also had several other inquiries about these puppies. She informed me that she felt I was just the type of owner every breeder strives to place their puppies with, and that if I could come either that day or the next morning, I would have my choice of the two females. We settled on the following morning, and after getting directions for the two and a half hour drive, she reported that she knew which of the two pups would be just right for us, and that she was anxious to see if we did indeed choose that pup.

The remainder of that day was spent preparing for the drive and the possibility of bringing home a new puppy. As we compiled two days of household chores into one, Wayne was full of questions and his excitement grew throughout the day. So did my own. We talked about potential names for the new pup and decided to stick with the same theme as Zippy's name, going to the next line in the song, "my, oh, my, what a wonderful day." Since we also, joked around calling Zip, an Oscar Meyer Wiener Dog, the new name had to fit in with that moniker as well. Finally, after much thought and deliberation, we came up with Maya as the name, and decided that if we had a hard time choosing between the two pups, we would see if either responded, in any way, when called Maya. Our last chore for the day was to load the car with supplies for decorating a float that the agility club was entering in the local Christmas parades. We were to spend Sunday afternoon completing the float. We would go look at the puppies, then go directly to the barn, where the float was being stored and worked on.

Sunday morning, we rose at seven and were out the door and on our way by eight. Zippy quickly found the basket and blanket in the backseat. We had brought them along, just in case there was a new puppy with us on our return. He settled himself in for a ride. Two and a half hours later, we found the breeder's home, parked in front of the garage and got Zip out of the car. As we walked toward the house, I saw three separate dog pens; each housing a single dachshund, another holding a pair of dachshunds, and the final pen, containing some sort of spaniel. All three pens were clean, had clean food and water available to the dogs, and were well constructed. The dogs all looked well cared for, healthy, and were friendly when we approached. The small house and its surrounding area were neat and tidy. Wayne held Zippy's leash at the edge of the enclosed entryway, while I approach the door. Before I could knock on the door, it opened to reveal an older lady, holding a small black and tan ball of fur.

She steps out onto the entryway as I introduce myself, Wayne and Zippy. While she introduces herself, my eyes, are drawn, to the pup in her arms, who is then held out to me, with the explanation,

"This is the pup, I think will be a good fit for your family, see what you think of her."

At first touch, it is apparent; the pup has just been bathed, and is still slightly damp. I sit down on a bench and begin to carefully examine the pup. Her eyes are clear and bright, the gums are pink, teeth are white and straight, nose is cool and damp, ears are clean and have no odor, fur is soft and glossy, and belly is not hard and distended. I run my hands down her back, tail and legs, feeling no lumps or abnormal areas. On feeling the top of her head, there are several small rough spots, pulling the fur back reveals these to be tiny scabs.

"What are these little scabs from?" I ask the breeder.

"Those are from her brothers, they get pretty

rough sometimes, when they play."
Okay, that's an understandable explanation. I have seen puppies play and they do sometimes get rather rough, even causing each other to yip.

"Why haven't the dew claws been removed?" is my next question.

"I leave that up to the new owner. Some people prefer to leave the dew claws intact."

Also I think to myself, an understandable explanation, in some circumstances. I don't know many cases where a small housedog would be left with dew claws intact, I thought they actually are a liability, easily snagged and torn on ordinary household furniture and carpeting. Perhaps there are still people who actually do use their dachshund for their intended hunting purposes, going into badger holes. Our area of West Virginia is not obviously populated with a nuisance badger population. I would choose to remove the dew claws since, should she come home with us, she will live inside as a member of the family.

I am pleased that this pup appears to be physically healthy and well cared for, so now I begin to appraise her personality and response to new experiences. So far she has tolerated all of my handling very well and now as I hold her up, she makes direct eye contact with me and pricks her ears forward when I talk to her. She shows no distress when cuddled and hugged. I take her over to meet Zippy. She wags her tail and shows submissive behavior. Zip is definitely interested and begins to play bow and pounce at her. She responds readily and soon they are romping about at our feet.

Now comes the real test, how does she act with Wayne. He sits down on the bench. I place the puppy in his arms. Being the mother hen that I am, with only one chick, I watch very closely the interaction between them. The pup turns her head toward him, gazes at him briefly with her soft brown eyes and promptly licks the end of his nose, eliciting a giggle from Wayne and smiles from myself as well as the breeder. The attraction between the two of them is instantly obvious and hard to ignore. He kissing the top of her head and fingering her soft silky ears, she licking his nose, ears, neck and anywhere else her little pink tongue can reach. Zippy has been standing on his hind legs watching every move this pup makes and he shows no concern for her being in Wayne's lap. There was only one more test to do. While Wayne is holding the pup, I call out the name we had already chosen "Maya." The pup turns her head and looks directly at me with curiosity. Done deal. This is our pup. The breeder, for whatever reason, now asks if I want to see the other puppy as well.

"No," I reply. "This is the one meant for us. If you don't mind, we came with cash and will take her home with us today."

I could not have asked for a better match to

what I had envisioned. She had such a life force and presence about her, she truly was irresistible. Her black and tan fur was softer and silkier than I had imagined it would be. Her chocolate brown eyes were full of an impish glint and she had the cutest little button nose. I could not help but to compare her to a living, breathing "Beanie Baby" dog. She may well have been the model from which the stuffed toy was designed.

While the breeder and I filled out the paperwork and settled up on the $450.00 payment, Wayne continues to hold the puppy while Zip watches intently. We are given a new puppy packet containing; puppy food, vaccination records, CKC registration papers and a new squeaky toy. The breeder explains that the puppies have not learned how to squeak the toys yet, too which Wayne supplies his only comment during the visit, "Oh, Zippy will teach her how to do that real quick, he is really good at it."

I am glancing through her papers during this time and see that her date of birth is listed as the day before Wayne's birthday, what a neat coincidence.

My final question for the breeder, "Does she get car sick?"

The breeder gives me a puzzled look and replies, "I don't know. She has never been in a car. I give them their shots and worm pills here. She has never been off the property."

Having finished our business, the breeder walks with us to our car. I hear several dogs begin to bark from behind her garage and turning my head in that direction wonder to myself if they are hers or a neighbor's. At that same moment, the breeder thanks me again and reports she really needs to get on the road for that wedding, turns and heads back toward her home. I open the car door for Zippy, who jumps up into the backseat, always eager for a car ride. When I tuck the puppy into her blanket lined basket beside him, he begins to roll his eyes and look uncertain. It appears he was fine and dandy playing with this little upstart, but sharing his car is a whole other thing all together. As we back out the driveway and turn onto the road, I tell Wayne to keep a close eye on the dogs for me. We leave the community, get back on the highway and within thirty minutes, I begin to hear that distinct "uurp, uurp," sound of a dog being sick.

"Mom, the puppy's throwing up all over her basket! Oh, yuck! It's really gross." wails Wayne, almost in a panic.

"It's okay son. We'll pull over. I'll clean it up and we'll let her calm down a little before we head back toward home." I try to respond as calmly as possible hoping not to escalate the level of distress in the car any further.

There is no hope of cleaning up the basket by the side of the road. Surprisingly, the blanket remained clean. The float decorations are moved from the trunk to the backseat. The soiled basket placed in the trunk. The puppy wrapped in the blanket and placed on Wayne's lap. Zippy maintains his usual spot in the backseat, we are ready to try this again. I explain to Wayne that this is all new to her and very overwhelming for such a little pup.

Thankfully being in Wayne's lap calms her down significantly and while there is some whining and rolling eyes, no more car sickness. We all begin to relax and Wayne talks nonstop about a multitude of new puppy related topics for the next hour. Suddenly I am shocked to hear another very distinct sound coming from behind our car, a police siren. A quick glance in the rear view mirror confirms... yep there it is, right behind me, a police cruiser, lights and siren going. I pull over onto the shoulder and watch in the mirror hoping it will go around me and continue on down the highway. That is not the case today, the cruiser matches my movement, also pulling over onto the shoulder and coming to a stop right behind my car. With my stomach feeling as if it is now sitting in my throat, I reach over to get the proof of insurance and registration out of the glove box and my license out of my wallet, telling Wayne not to worry. I have all my papers ready when the officer arrives at my already lowered window. He smiles warmly at me then asks, "Do you know how fast you were driving?"

I don't know when I glanced at the speedometer last, so I just as warmly reply, "I honestly have no idea, how fast I was going." Figuring, I might as well be honest and admit to my own lack of diligence.

"Well, Ma'am, you were doing 83 in a 55 miles per hour zone. Were you being distracted by something?"

I am feeling rather sheepish now. I truly had no sense that I was going that fast. It's not something I normally do. I am usually a very conscientious driver. Thinking on it, I don't recall seeing any speed limit signs that normally prompt me to look at my speedometer. Most of our state highways have a speed limit of 70, and I guess I was unconsciously thinking this road was the same.

"Yes, officer, I was distracted. We just got this new puppy and we were talking about her. I am sorry, I have traveled this road several times before and I never realized the speed limit here was 55."

"What did you think the speed limit was?" the officer questions, still with the same warm smile.

"70," I reply. "Like the other highways in the state."

"Even if it was 70 mph, you still would have been speeding."

Ouch, the truth hurts... $150's worth of hurt. Still smiling, the officer hands me the ticket, then asks about all the stuff in the back seat. I explain it is for decorating a float; we had it in the trunk, the puppy threw up on the basket we had her in, no way to clean it up along the side of the road, put the dirty basket in the trunk, moved all the decorations into the back seat, and here we are. He gives me a little chuckle saying,

"Sounds like a tough day so far. Maybe if you watch your speed for the rest of your trip, it might make things a little better for you."

The officer then leans down, looks at the puppy in Wayne's lap and tells him,

"That sure is a cute puppy. You enjoy her now."

I do indeed watch my speed carefully for the remainder of the trip and by the time we pull up to the barn, everybody else is already there and working on the float. While I am cleaning up Maya's soiled basket, the other club members are passing her around cuddling her and exclaiming on how adorable she is. After unloading the decorations from the car, I tuck Maya back into her now clean basket, leaving Zippy loose to freely explore the barn. I then start on decorating the float. Maya never whimpers. She watches the activity for a few minutes, then curls up in her basket and falls sound asleep. Over the next three hours, we all peek in on her every so often, while we complete the decorating. I have to wake her up after we are done with the float to do her business. Maya roams around for a little bit, looking at each person as she comes to them, showing no concern at being petted. Right after she does her business, she spies Zippy trotting around the agility ring and she is off like a flash after him, following every step he makes. Zip turns, gives her a brief glance, then goes back to his mission without another look at his new shadow. Maya continues to follow him step for step and sniff for sniff.

While the dogs are roaming about, we are confirming the parade dates, times and locations we will all be participating in with our dogs. We agree that the small dogs and their owners will ride on the float. The big dogs will walk alongside their owners who will be handing out candy. Wayne will play the role of the train conductor, on the train engine shaped float. This time when Maya joins us in the car, Zippy does not roll his eyes or show any sign of concern, he just settles in for another car ride.

Upon arriving at home, I carry Maya into the house set her on the floor and carefully watch Zip's reaction to this intruder in his home. Maya explores the downstairs area of the house, with Zip sitting back at a distance watching. He shows no concern, even when she finds his basket of toys and begins to pull them out one by one. I feel pleased, this seems to be going very well at this point anyway... it is still early and a new experience for all of us.

Feeding time proves to be a little difficult. Zip decides he prefers Maya's puppy chow over his own food. She gives him a couple of warning growls, which he ignores, and sticks his nose right into her dish anyway. Maya gives him a quizzical look, then almost as if shrugging her shoulders in despair, turns and starts to eat the food in his dish. They obviously came to an understanding, but from my point of view, this is not going to work. I pick up both food dishes, put Zip outside and then put Maya's food back down for her to eat. When she has finished, I reverse the process going outside with Maya, while Zip eats his food. I will need to come up with a better routine at feeding time; otherwise it is going to be a long nine months while Maya is on puppy food.

As I am outside with Maya, I notice she seems to be very fearful and uncertain in the yard. She is hesitant to explore and startles at the normal sounds of a small town community... cars going by, kids yelling and laughing, other dogs barking and even the dried leaves on the ground. I'll need to stay outside with her until she learns what to do out here and becomes accustomed to the noises around her. I will also need to keep an eye on that little bit of resource guarding she displayed with her food.

Wayne and I eat supper, clean up the kitchen, put our pajama's on and then sit on the couch watching the two dogs start to play a game of tug with a knotted rope toy. After watching them for about twenty minutes, I casually and without thought, turn the TV on. Maya instantly reacts. She lets out a yip, looks around nervously, with rolling eyes and then darts under a chair where she crouches down and shakes from head to toe.

"What happened, Mom? Why is she hiding under the chair?" Wayne wonders out loud.

"I don't know, son. They were playing nicely together... then all of a sudden she just quit."

I coax her out from under the chair, set her on the couch with us and pet her while we watch TV. Zippy jumps up and lies down nearby watching her out of the corner of his eye. I feel Maya start to relax. As I watch her, I notice she is glancing toward the TV and then quickly looking away. Wait a minute; surely she is not afraid of the TV. I turn it off and watch as she still glances in that direction, but is not shaking anymore. When I turn it back on she starts to shake again and turns her head away.

"Well, for Pete's sake. I think she is afraid of the TV."

"What?" Wayne asks, as stunned as I am.

"Let's turn the volume way down, see if that helps."

I turn it down, until it is barely audible to us and wait. Maya glances back and forth between the TV and Zip, who is asleep a few inches away. This continues for a few minutes then she lays her head down. I wait a little while then turn the volume up a couple of clicks. She looks at the TV again, over at Zip, who hasn't moved then lays her head back down again. I slowly repeat this process until the volume is at normal level. By the last increase, Maya doesn't even look up. Wayne and I look at each other and shrug. That was odd.

The TV program we are watching ends, and it is time for Wayne to go up to bed. He gives Maya a kiss on the top of her head, tells her "Goodnight baby girl." He gives Zip a pat on the top of his head, gives me my usual hug, then declares...

"I'm glad we got a new puppy Mom, thank you. She really is cute, even if she acts a little weird."

"She'll get used to everything pretty quick and then she won't be so weird." I respond.

I take Maya back outside to do her business, carrying her both up and down the three steps off the back porch. Not only are her legs too short to navigate the steps, she is so close to the ground it is difficult to see when she actually squats to do her business. This time, she seems a little less hesitant. She actually has her nose to the ground and is exploring an area about two feet away from me. I walk out into the yard a few more feet she follows still with her nose to the ground. She then appears to squat for a few seconds, I'm not sure, but I think she did. I wait a few more minutes and after she only sniffs around a little more, I decide she must have done her business and we head back into the warmth of the house.

Both dogs settle back down on the couch with me to watch a little more TV. When just a few minutes have passed, the phone rings and as I answer it, I see Maya is back under the chair shaking and rolling her eyes. The phone too, seriously, has she never heard these things before? The call is from our town's Mayor informing me the city clerk has taken ill. I was needed to fill in while she was off, it would probably be for the entire week.

"I'll be there" is my answer.

All right now, here I am with a new puppy, which appears to be rather nervous so far, needs to go for her first vet visit, called in to cover a full work week and Wayne returning back to school after the holiday break. I settle myself back on the couch watching Maya but leaving her to figure out on her own it is safe to come out from under the chair. Zip and I relax to finish watching the program I had gotten interested in. Sure enough, it does not take long before Maya is standing on her hind legs looking at me with pleading eyes to be allowed back on the couch. I lift her up and she settles herself against my leg and falls asleep.

The program over I decide I had better wrap things up for the night, as I will have to get up earlier tomorrow to be at the office on time. I drag the cat's old carrier down from the attic, wipe it out and line it with a towel and spend time introducing Maya to the carrier. Having sold Zip's old and unused training crate (that he so obviously hated) at a yard sale, this carrier would have to do. It was actually a rather large one that had accommodated two thirteen pound cats at the same time. It was plenty spacious enough for a three or four pound puppy. I sit on the floor in front of the carrier with Maya by my side, give her a little treat, then place another treat just inside the door of the carrier. She walks right in, grabs the treat, sits down in the carrier and eats it. I tell her, "good girl" while I rub her ears. When she walks back out of the carrier, I put another treat further back in. Again, she walks right in and sits down to eat the treat. This time I close the door, tell her "good girl" and then open the door for her to come back out. She stays in the carrier looking at me rather proudly. I close the door again. This time I walk out of the room for a minute, then return, open the door; give her rubs and another "good girl." She seems to be quite comfortable in the carrier and shows no sign of distress.

Zippy has not forgotten what this type of device is for, he tries watching briefly, but as soon as he sees Maya go into the carrier, he rolls his eyes, then quietly makes his way upstairs where he climbs into his dog bed. He wants no part of this business and puts as much distance between himself and the offending object as possible. I am pleasantly surprised at Maya's acceptance of the carrier and feel confident that she will be just fine while we are out of the house for school and work.

Maya and I follow Zip upstairs to get ready for bed. I put an old pillow on the floor beside my bed for her to sleep on and cover her with a small blanket. Zip sits in his bed, watching with great curiosity this new night time routine. He has a preference for sleeping under a blanket, so after settling Maya into her new bed, I do the same thing I do every night before climbing into bed myself, spread Zip's blanket over him. Satisfied that both dogs are settled in, I finally crawl into my own bed and hope there will not be too much whining this first night of Maya's life with us. Only a few minutes have passed when I hear Maya padding around the bedroom. I sit up and watch her head right over to Zippy's dog bed, push her nose under the blanket and climb into "his" bed with him. Zip protests with a soft, brief growl (a sound rarely heard from him), pops his head up giving me a look, as if to say, "It's in my bed, get it out!" I merely watch and wait to see what happens next. Maya doesn't budge, or even bat an eye. After looking around helplessly for a bit, Zip puts his nose back under the blanket, curls up and both dogs are fast asleep in a matter of minutes. They stay that way for the entire night.

Monday morning, after a surprisingly quiet night, it is time for breakfast and I need to find a way to keep Zip from eating Maya's puppy chow. I put

Maya in the laundry room with her food and put a baby gate across the doorway (the same baby gate that could not contain Zip in his puppyhood days), and am met with success. Maya eats her food. Zip watches from the other side of the doorway. When Maya has finished eating, I take her outside one last time, then before leaving the house for school and work, I open the door to the training crate placing a treat inside. Maya walks right in, eats the treat and calmly sits down. As I close the crate door, I can't help remembering, how terrible it was putting Zip in there when he was a pup.

During my lunch break, I return back home, anxious to see how Maya is dealing with the reality of being in the crate for an extended amount of time. As I open the front door, Zippy is not asleep on the couch, his normal spot when left alone, he comes trotting out from the dining room where Maya is positioned in her crate. He paces excitedly from me to the crate as if encouraging me, to get her out of there. I need not have worried, other than a little spot of piddle, Maya has done just fine. Both dogs are let outside together. I watch from the kitchen window, as I prepare myself some lunch. I notice that Maya is following Zip around the yard, not looking as nervous as she was yesterday. I have a few minutes to play with the dogs after eating my lunch, so I throw Zip's tennis ball from room to room for him to fetch and expend a bit of energy. Maya is intrigued and amused by this new activity and she begins to follow Zip each time he runs after the ball. She just isn't fast enough yet, to beat him to the ball.

I repeat the same routine to put her back into the crate. She enters the crate voluntarily and then calmly sits down. The afternoon results are also the same a little piddle, that's it. I can't believe how easily she is accepting the crate; it sure makes for a less stressful morning.

Now that work and school are over, we take Maya for her first visit to our vet to activate her health guarantee and get her rabies shot. Once in the exam room, Dr. Kendrick begins to examine Maya carefully from head to toe, while asking questions about the breeder she came from. He acknowledges that he is familiar with her as a breeder and hadn't realized that she was still breeding, as he has not had any new puppies of hers as patients for a few years. I then point out the scabs on the top of Maya's head, relating the breeder's explanation. Dr. Kendrick confirms they could be consistent with rough puppy play. He then notes that she is slightly dehydrated and advises me to make sure she knows where the water bowl is and that she does indeed drink from it. In general, she presents as a healthy, nice looking pup. We then discuss having her spayed and her dew claws removed at the same time.

"How is Zippy taking to her so far? Any signs he is having trouble adjusting to her?" questions the doctor.

"He rolled his eyes a few times, tried to eat her puppy chow and growled at her once when she climbed into his dog bed. I separated them at feeding time and the other issues, they resolved themselves, peaceably." I respond.

"Well, that's a pretty mild reaction from a male who has been the only dog in the house for years. Do you have any other concerns or questions for me?"

I relate Maya's unusual reactions to the various normal household items she has been exposed to so far. He agrees that is not typical behavior at her age and we should be aware in the future that new experiences may be stressful for her, before discussing possible ways to acclimate her to these items as well as any other anxiety provoking items or circumstances. I thank Dr. Kendrick for his advice and on our way out I schedule her spay and dew claw removal surgery.

The same training routine is continued through the week. Maya is starting to settle in well. She glances at the TV when it is on, but no longer hides under the chair and she does not react to the telephone at all now. On Wednesday evening it is time for Zip's agility class. Maya goes along for the social interaction and to become more familiar with the environment. During the class, Wayne holds Maya while Zip and I take our turns running the course. Several club members pet and hold her throughout the hour. When the class is over Maya is set down where she gets to meet the other dogs, under supervision. There are no signs of aggression or fear. She gives each dog a little sniff and then goes about her own business, which is following Zip.

By the time the work week is over, I am pretty tired, but know that we have a parade to participate in on Saturday morning. I need to do a quick house cleaning on Friday evening. I start sweeping the kitchen floor and am surprised when Maya begins to bark and growl at the broom as it moves across the floor. At first I try to just ignore the behavior, but then she starts to lunge at the broom. I firmly tell her "NO" and continue to sweep. She steps back briefly, but then lunges again. This time I lay the broom down on the floor waiting until she hesitantly approaches it, sniffs it thoroughly and then walks away before I pick the broom back up. As soon as the broom begins to move again, she starts barking and lunging. I have got to finish this so, I keep sweeping telling her "NO" every time she lunges until the chore is finished. Next chore is to mop the kitchen floor. Anticipating the same behavior, I first lay the mop and bucket on the floor, giving Maya the opportunity to familiarize herself to the items. Even though she has no reaction to the inert items, as soon as I begin moving the mop across the floor, the barking and lunging begins again. I practice the same correction every time she reacts and ultimately, the floor also gets mopped.

Now, I need to run the vacuum cleaner. I wonder what the reaction to this will be. Going through the same drill, letting her investigate the machine before turning it on, doesn't really seem to make a difference. She barks, growls, lunges and actually tries to bite the vacuum cleaner when it moves across the floors. This is just too frustrating. It takes longer to complete the chore when you have a three and a half pound puppy attacking your tools. Yet, it is also funny, because you have a three and a half pound puppy attacking your tools. If things continue this way, I'll need to start a list of issues to work on with Maya.

The Christmas season is about to begin in earnest with the first of three parades now upon us. It turns out it is forecast to be rather cold. Wayne and I dress in multiple layers in preparation and take two heavy blankets along to wrap the dogs in. Zippy has always loved going to watch parades, he is particularly fond of the drums in the marching bands, and I am confident that he will be fine. Maya however, with her reactions to some of the things at home, is a concern. We all load up on the float as it is positioned in the line-up and as we are waiting to begin, get settled into our particular spots. I wrap Maya up in one blanket, set her on my lap, wrap the other blanket around Zip and sit him to my side right next to his girlfriend Annie, a pretty little Maltese. The parade starts; we slowly begin to make our way along the route. The noise and excited atmosphere intensifies as we proceed. Zip is enjoying himself, looking around and showing no sign of fear or nervousness. I am pleasantly surprised to see that Maya is also looking around curiously and is showing no sign of fear or anxiety. I am thrilled; she is becoming comfortable and confident in her new life and all of the experiences we are offering her.

Maya has been with us for one week now. She is adjusting fairly well and we have all bonded strongly with her. Sundays are our day for family dinner at the grandparents' house. Zip always goes along and enjoys it immensely. He romps and plays with their four Yorkies and also seems to unerringly, find something to get into, that he shouldn't. This will be Maya's first visit and her chance to meet most of the family, human and canine alike. One of the Yorkies, Teddy tends to be snappy and short tempered with other dogs. Zip has learned, unfortunately the hard way, to give Teddy a very wide berth at all times. Due to Maya's small size, I keep her either on my lap or right by my side, when she is not being held by someone else that is, for the entire visit. She does very well... being tolerant and open to all the family members holding her at different times and showing an interest in the other dogs. I'm sure given Teddy's behavior in the past, she will ultimately have a run in with him but, I'll hold off on that as long as possible. At least until she is more equal in size and less likely to be injured.

Thank goodness the coming week allows us to get back to our normal schedule. Monday morning Zip and Maya both ride along to drop Wayne off at school. This has been part of Zip's daily routine for the past four years. He likes watching the kids come and go and the occasional attention when someone comes over to the car to pet him. In other situations he is protective of "his" car, but not at school. This will be the first day since Maya joined our family that Wayne will not be home with us. She bonded with him from the first day, when she laid on his lap, all the way home. She has already decided her spot in the car is on his lap. She shows no interest in sitting in the back seat with Zip. We arrive at school; Wayne hands Maya over to me, gets his book bag and exit's the car. Maya wiggles, whines and tries to follow Wayne. After he shuts the car door, Zip jumps up into the now empty seat, stands on his hind legs and watches Wayne and the other kids entering the school. I set Maya in the seat with Zip. She also stands up on her hind legs to watch out the window. It doesn't appear she can actually see out the window, she is too short. I pick her back up and hold her up high enough to see out the window. She catches sight of Wayne waving at us and starts to wiggle and whine again. We watch until he disappears through the doors, before we pull out onto the street and back toward home.

On school days I usually wait until getting back home to prepare breakfast for myself sometimes, taking the easy way out and doing a McDonald's drive-thru instead. Today is one of those days. I place my order and pull up to the window. Zip climbs onto my lap and waits at the car window, looking for his favorite worker, the one that gives him a piece of bacon on occasion and always a pat on the head. I hold Maya up to the window so she can see what this place is all about. Her nose is quivering like a rabbit's, so many wonderful smells. Sure enough, Zip's favorite worker comes to the window holding a piece of bacon for him. She leans out handing the bacon to Zip, then sees Maya.

As she is giving Zip his pat on the head (the bacon, having already disappeared) she exclaims, "Oh, you got a new puppy! How adorable. Is it a dachshund too?"

"Yes, she is a long-haired dachshund. Her name is Maya and we got her a week ago." I respond. Maya first sniffs intently at Zip's muzzle, learning the enticing scent of that piece of bacon, that was gone too quickly for her to experience, and then sniffing at the hand that held the bacon. She shows no fear over that hand as it reaches over to pet her, even gives it a little lick. The bacon, I'm sure, is the root of this interest. More of the workers have come over to the window now and as they are admiring Wayne's new puppy, one of them asks if the puppy can have a piece of bacon too.

"No, we better wait until she gets a little older before you all go spoiling her too." They all laugh at that, a little sheepishly as I get my order, place the bag on the floor, and drive away from the window. Before I can pull back onto the street, Maya is trying to stick her nose into the bag. I lean over and fold the top of the bag down tightly for the ride home. A memory flashes through my mind of Zip and I, driving on the highway to go pick Wayne up from a weekend visit to Grandpa's. I had gone through another McDonald's drive-thru on the way and had set my french fries in the cup holder between the two front seats. I eat my hamburger then reach to grab a couple of fries, only to discover that the box is half empty. While I was eating the burger, Zip was eating the fries, right under my nose and until then, undetected. Maya will have a harder time getting away with things like that. Zip has already been there and done that and I have five years of experience with a wiener dog under my belt now.

Back at the house I settle down with my breakfast, the newspaper and the Today Show. Zip takes up his usual position, about a foot away, waiting patiently, for something to either fall or be shared. Over this past week, Maya has figured out that waiting right beside Zip is a good place to be. Of course with a kid in the house, it does pay off sometimes. This morning, it does not. After I finish eating, Maya gets her puppy chow and then goes outside to potty. She is starting to understand the concept and I give Zip a lot of credit. She watches every move he makes and then copies his actions, exactly. If he sniffs a clump of grass, she sniffs it. If he rolls on the floor, she rolls on the floor. When he goes potty, she does too. This seems to be an excellent method. She is so far training much easier than Zip did.

Time to get on with my day. I don't have to go into the office today, so the plan is to work on one of the many on-going remodeling projects here at the house, then spend time working with Maya on her manners and basic obedience. The work goes well and by lunch time, I have done all that I can for now. The weather is fairly warm today, a good opportunity to start leash training. Maya has proven to be observant of Zippy's reactions to things she is unsure of. Let's take advantage of that. First I put Zippy's collar on him, let Maya sniff her new collar, gently brush it all over her body then loosely put it on her. There is no significant reaction; she turns around in circles a few times, scratches at it a few more times before pouncing at Zip playfully. He is pacing from me to the door and back in excited anticipation of either a walk or a car ride somewhere fun. Next step, I snap his leash on letting him walk around dragging it. Maya watches his leash for a second and then proceeds to grab it in her mouth and pull. Zip is confused and tries to go back to the door, but Maya is tugging at him with all of her now four pound might, too funny. Let's give him a break. Snapping Maya's leash on her does distract her attention from him. Now she has her own leash in her mouth and is trotting around the living room as proud as a peacock. I can't help but laugh at her; she is so adorably full of herself. I pick her up, remove the leash from her mouth, take hold of Zip's leash and head out the door.

We walk down the street this way for a short while and then I set Maya down, grab hold of her leash and begin walking again. The first few steps are okay, but as I expected, when Maya reaches the end of her leash length and feels that resistance, she begins to struggle. Zip and I take a step forward, wait for her to follow then take another step, wait again, until we reach the end of the street. Not too bad, she is no longer struggling against the leash; she just sits down when she feels the resistance. The same method on the way back up the street proves to be successful. By the time we reach the house, she is walking slowly but steadily along. Another few trips back and forth, she is beginning to keep up with our normal pace. I must look rather comical right now I think. As I am walking up and down the street, I have two dogs going at opposite speeds and am therefore walking with one arm extended way out in front to accommodate Zip's pace and the other extended way out behind me to accommodate Maya's.

Another small meal of puppy chow, a potty break, and Maya is exhausted. She curls up in the dog bed and takes a nap. Zip takes advantage of the reprieve and gets some solo cuddle time with me on the couch. Maya eventually wakes up and after another trip outside, we begin manners training. My biggest concern was her food guarding. Even though it is rather mild now, I know this behavior can escalate to serious proportions over time if not addressed. I sit on the floor beside her food dish with a handful of puppy chow closing my hand so she can smell the food, but not get to it. I wait while she sniffs my hand, paws at it, circles around it and when she finally sits down in puzzlement, I drop a piece of food into her dish. She eats that piece and we repeat the process until the handful is gone. According to my research, this method is supposed to teach the puppy that good things happen when a human hand is over the food dish and that sitting calmly also brings good things. We will practice this every day at every meal, until she no longer shows any negative behavior.

The last thing to work on today is Maya's issues with the broom, mop and vacuum cleaner. After the conversation with our vet and some additional research, I think I have a pretty good plan to modify this behavior. I really don't want food to be her only reward during training so I have been watching to see what else might be a good motivator or distraction for her. She is showing a great interest in Zip's tennis ball and is already racing after it when I throw it for Zip. This might prove to be just the right motivation for her. First I take the broom, lay it on the kitchen floor, sit down next to it and call Maya over to my lap. As before, she does not react to the unmoving broom. With one hand, I start to move the broom across the floor and get the reaction I was waiting for, she starts to bark and lunge toward the broom. Before she gets off my lap, I toss the tennis ball directly past her nose and away from the broom. Success, she turns away from the broom and goes after the ball. While she plays with the ball, I keep moving the broom. It becomes very obvious she is torn between the two items and the temptation proves to be too much, back she comes toward the broom. This time another ball is rolled past her. Works again, she goes after the second ball. We repeat this exercise a few more times with good results each time. I decide to only work on the broom for now. When she masters the broom, then we can expand to the mop and hopefully, eventually move on to the vacuum cleaner. No sense in overwhelming her by moving too quickly with too many items.

It's time to go pick Wayne up from school. Both dogs go along for the ride. We pull up to the school and Zip assumes his usual position of standing on his hind legs, watching out the window. Maya tries to emulate, but still needs a boost. Most of the kids have come out and so far, no Wayne. When he does finally come out of the school doors, Maya starts to wiggle, whine and hop up and down on my lap. It is almost as if she is thinking, "my boy, my boy, hurray, he came back." Poor Wayne, Maya is so excited to have him back, he barely gets in the car before he is assaulted with untold puppy kisses. I watch him laugh hysterically, when there is a tap on the car window. One of Wayne's teachers is there, also watching the unrestrained love between a boy and his puppy. Through my laughter induced tears, I put the car window down.

"Wayne told me he got a new puppy. I saw her reaction when he got in the car and had to come over and see her close-up." the teacher is also laughing at Maya's antics.

Wayne holds Maya up and as he is telling his teacher all about the new pup, two more teachers come over and admire her as well. Zip watches this for a brief minute and then decides... he needs in on this action too. He jumps into Wayne's lap and positions himself right beside Maya. Now they both get the attention from the group of teachers at our car window. Finally we are able to head back home and today's enthusiastic reaction from Maya, upon Wayne's return from school, proves to be a daily occurrence for the next four and a half years that never fails to bring a smile to both our faces and comes to be known as the "Kissy Wiggle."

Later that week, Zip goes to the vet to have his teeth cleaned. His teeth have just a slight tilt to them and the tartar builds up rather quickly, requiring an annual cleaning under sedation. Maya is left at home in her crate while Zip and I drop Wayne off at school, then go to the vet's office where he is left in their capable hands, until this afternoon. A quick run into the local department store, then back home, where Maya and I get down to some serious girl time. First we each enjoy a long, hot, uninterrupted bubble bath (bubbles, for me anyway, not for Maya). Then we blow-dry our hair. Maya isn't overly fond of the blow-dryer, so she mostly gets a towel dry. Next we style our hair, which is a good brushing for Maya, and finally she gets little red bows in her ears... too adorable. Bright colors definitely work well for her, she absolutely looks like a little girl with her hair up in pigtails. Now that we are all dolled up, we have to go somewhere. I decide to take her out visiting around town. After we do drive-thru for lunch, we stop in at my hairdresser, who is also a dachshund owner. I take Maya in to the shop where Lisa has just finished up with a customer. She holds Maya for a while, admiring her bows and chatting. All three of us head outside onto her shops little porch, where Lisa hands Maya back over to me. We chat for a little bit longer and as the other customer is leaving, she reaches over to pet Maya. Unexpectedly, Maya growls, and actually snaps at the elderly lady who is trying to pet her. Through my shock, I am still able to respond quickly with a harsh, "Aach, No." I apologize to the woman, who is thankfully, not upset by the reaction. When she has left, Lisa and I look at each other, shaking our heads "Where did that come from?" she asks.

"I don't know. It's not like she hasn't been held and petted by strangers before today."

"She was perfectly fine, when I held her." Lisa notes. "Maybe there is just something about that particular person she didn't like."

"It could be, but I'll make sure to pay more attention to her reactions to new people, before they try to pet her." I reply.

Our next stop is the post office. After an uneventful greeting by the post-mistress, we head over to town hall. I sort through the work I have for tomorrow and while there, Maya sits quietly in my lap. She is quickly learning what Zip already knows, this is a good place to visit, good rubs from the clerk and sometimes even a treat. Each time a customer comes in and is waited on by the town clerk, Maya pops her head up and watches intently. Several customers notice her and ask to see her. Maya still has her bows in her ears and acts as if she knows how cute she looks, sitting primly on the counter while being admired and sometimes petted. She has no further negative reactions to anybody else who pets her today. It is almost time for school to let out and since I have to run in to the school's office, we leave a little early.

At the school, I carry Maya with me up to the main office. It is too soon to leave her in the car unattended. I feel the need to make this a quick visit, classes will let out soon and the hallways will become the scene of a middle school stampede soon. At the office, the secretary sees me enter asking, "Is this Wayne's new puppy I have heard so much about?"

"Yes, this is Maya. If you would hold her, I can sign those IEP papers now."

"Sure, I have them right here." she responds.
I begin signing in all the marked places and the secretary is fingering Maya's ears as she comments, "I didn't know that dachshunds came with long hair. Where did you get her?"

I give her the location and name of the breeder, relating what our vet had disclosed and our experience in dealing with her. "I'll have Wayne bring you one of her cards tomorrow then you can contact her if you're interested in a puppy."

"My husband and I have been talking about getting a little house dog, but couldn't agree on what breed. He wants a dachshund and I want a dog with long hair. This is a breed we can both have what we want." she explains; then asks, "Were there more puppies in her litter?"

"I know there was at least one more female still there when we picked out Maya and the breeder had made reference to a couple of males also from the same litter. I don't know if any of them are still there, but you can find out tomorrow after Wayne brings you the phone number. I better get going, I'm not sure, Maya is ready to handle the chaos in the hallways after the bell rings."

Maya and I are now trying to make a quick exit through the halls. We don't quite make it. We are nearly to the doors when the bell rings. Maya startles in my arms and looks around a bit wildly. I tuck her inside my coat while we wade through the swarming mass of noisy middle-school students just released from their day of confinement. We do manage to beat the worst of the stampede and meet Wayne at the car. As soon as we are all settled into our seats, Maya begins her "kissy wiggle."

Proceeding straight to the vet's office, Wayne

and Maya, wait in the car while I go in to pick up Zip. I meet with the doctor and get Zip's aftercare instructions. He tolerated his procedure very well and other than being a little groggy and sore; he should have no problems, reports the doctor. Little does he know how difficult it will be to get the antibiotic pills into Zip for the ten days. For us, the ordeal is not over until the medication is finished. As soon as I lift Zippy up into the car, Maya is sniffing at his muzzle. She seems to understand that something is different. She is very calm with Zip, not trying to play. For the ride home and the rest of the evening while he sleeps, she curls herself up right beside him, watching him.

Just a matter of days after Zip's dental procedure, Maya is playing with a stuffed animal in the kitchen while I am washing dishes. I hear a gagging sound. Turning around; I see her pawing at her mouth and salivating excessively. Picking her up reveals she has managed to get a plastic eye off of the stuffed toy and wedged perfectly over one of her molars, just like a cap or crown. Several attempts to pull the eye off are unsuccessful. Her mouth is just too small to hold open with one hand and try to dislodge the eye with the other. Not to mention, she is still salivating excessively making everything slippery, and she is starting to panic as well. I realize this is going to take an extra pair of hands. Luckily my neighbor is home and while I use both hands to hold Maya's mouth open, he uses a paper towel to wipe off the eye and then gently pull it off her tooth. Problem solved, crisis averted. Maya gives his hand a little lick to show her gratitude. Once back at home, even though she has just had a little bit of a scare, she goes right back to the same stuffed animal starting to chew on the remaining plastic eye. Needless to say, that toy finds its way into the garbage can along with two more that have plastic eyes, from now on, only cloth or sewn eyes on the stuffed animals.

The next couple of weeks are busy with the usual holiday bustle of shopping, decorating, baking, Christmas parades and parties. Maya does very well with all the changes around the house. She is particularly fond of the Christmas tree, deciding it is her new favorite place to nap and stash her toys. When wrapped packages start to appear, she takes them as an intrusion, pushing the smaller ones out of her way and trying to squeeze past the larger ones. It becomes a daily shuffle of packages. I pile them neatly under the tree and she pushes them out into the middle of the floor. After a few days of this, we reach a compromise; I pile the packages under one side of the tree leaving the other side open for Maya to lie under. We are both satisfied.

One last shopping trip adds a few more packages under the tree. These prove to be quite different in Maya's opinion. No matter where I put them, they end up under "her" side of the tree and mysteriously, the corners of the packages start to become wet and frayed. HMMM. Now, how does such a young pup, one that has not experienced Christmas before, know that these packages came from the pet store? It might be a good idea to put these packages out of puppy reach for now.

The first snow of the season comes during the night a few days before Christmas and Maya's reaction is without a doubt, priceless. Her first step into this altered landscape elicits a fearful yip. A quick glance to me and Zip for reassurance gives her the courage to tentatively venture out into the yard. She does her business quickly before starting to explore. Luckily her first snow is only a few inches deep. That little bit is enough to reach up to her belly and as she begins to romp around, snow clings to her fur and forms snowballs on her legs, chest, belly and ends of her ears. By the time we head back inside, she has quite a collection attached to her. Standing in the middle of the kitchen, she becomes aware of these little snowballs dangling from the various parts of her body. She twists herself around this way and that, looking at them in a puzzled manner. Then begins to grab them in her mouth and pull them off of her legs one by one, dropping each offending object onto the floor then pouncing on it until it magically disappears before her eyes. This process is repeated until all of the snowballs have been removed or melted on their own. Winter here in West Virginia can be pretty brutal some years. Watching Maya experience the coming snows should prove to be great entertainment for all of us.

This year we will be spending Christmas with our family in Pennsylvania, so the day before we are to leave, we have an early gift opening for the dogs. Zippy is an old pro with wrapped presents. He leaves them alone until, we sit on the floor and place the present in front of him. At that moment, the present is fair game to him; he grabs it in his mouth, shakes it, claws at it, then uses his teeth to tear the paper off bit by bit, leaving a wonderful pile of soggy shredded paper strewn all around him. It doesn't take Maya long to pick up on this new activity. She joins in with such relish; we are reduced to boneless lumps from laughter. The absolute joy on her face, the inane silliness and her obvious pride over the rawhide bone (bigger than she), will prove to be one of those moments that etches itself in our minds for many years to come.

Each dog has received; a new bone, squeaky toy, bag of treats and dog Christmas Cookie, and jointly they now have a dog bed that will be big enough for both to sleep in when Maya is also full grown. Having opened all of their presents, Maya is now focused on her bone, but is carefully watching Zippy; go through his normal routine with a new squeaky toy. First, you scratch at the squeaker with the front paws until a hole is opened in the fabric of the toy, then remove the stuffing (one mouth full at a time), toss the stuffing over the shoulder, dislodge the squeaker, toss it over the shoulder as well, continue removing stuffing, until the toy is nothing but an empty shell. Then abandon it for all time, having successfully incapacitated it. This process usually takes about an hour, sometimes a toy may last a day or two, before he gets a hole chewed through the material, but not very often. With his toy sufficiently destroyed, Zip now lays down to join Maya in chewing on their rawhides. Shortly, he spies Maya's stuffed toy, starts to go for it and is met with a sharp bark from her, seemingly a warning, as she abandons her bone and stands over her stuffed toy possessively. She apparently has seen his treatment of stuffed toys and will not tolerate her toy meeting the same fate. Zip backs off and Maya picks up her toy, takes it over to where her bone is and then promptly lays down over top of both items, not taking her eyes off of Zip.

The stare down lasts for about ten minutes when he gives up and goes back to his bone. Maya continues to guard her "stuff" and Zip eventually gets tired of his bone. He crawls into the dog bed for a nap. Maya leaves her post, comes over to be lifted onto the couch, where she also starts to nap. A good twenty minutes later, there is a slight movement in the dog bed. Slowly; a nose pokes out from under the blanket, followed by one eye, then the other. No response from

Maya, who is sound asleep on the couch. Inch by slow motion inch Zip eases out of the dog bed creeping over to snatch up Maya's toy. Here his stealth ends. The squeaker is just too tempting. The sound of the first squeak brings Maya abruptly out of her slumber to the sight of "her" toy in Zip's destructive paws. She glances at me, back to Zip, then let's out a large sigh, laying her head back down in resignation, to observe the demise of her first Christmas toy.

The next morning, Zip knows something is up, the suitcases have been brought down from the attic, and the packing has begun. This activity always provokes a cautious, nervous excitement in him. Sometimes he goes with us to someplace new, but sometimes he goes to the vet to be boarded, in a cage he does not like. Being that it is winter time; the dogs will not be going with us. Nana has several large, older cats in the house that are not fond of dogs and will stay outside, until the dogs are gone. It is too cold for either the cats, or the dogs, to be outside for extended amounts of time. It is less stressful for everyone if the dogs are boarded. I am hopeful that Maya's presence will be a calming influence for Zip and that he will not scrape up his nose in the kennel this time. This behavior has been an ongoing pattern when he is boarded and has proven to be impossible to alter. If there is a mat, towel or blanket, in his kennel, he will obsessively push it around with his nose until his nose is scraped open. If all items are removed, he will push his nose under and between any parts of the kennel he can access to the same results. The staff has tried many things to stop this behavior to no avail and now is prepared to start ointment on his nose as soon as he starts rooting. We will see in a few days if Maya is indeed a calming influence for him.

Our trip has gone well. We had a wonderful time and as usual, the car is packed fuller on the trip home. We are anxious to get the dogs, get home, unpack the car and get back to our normal routine. At the vet's office both dogs are elated to see us and scramble their way up the aisle to greet us warmly. Maya does a frantic "kissy wiggle" routine, while Zip tries to climb up onto my shoulder as I check his nose, it is scraped, but much less than in the past. A vet tech hands me a little tube of ointment to continue treatment at home until the scrape is healed.

"How did they do?" I ask the tech.

"Zippy tried to do his rooting thing, but the little one thought this was a game and tried to play every time he started. She kept him distracted fairly well. We tried to feed them separately as you suggested but, neither one would eat until we put them together. They both ate well after that. Your little one sure is a sweetheart. We let them both out to play several times a day and she just had a blast every time."

So, it sounds like Maya did help ease Zippy's anxiety somewhat, that's a bit of a relief. Hopefully any future trips to the vet for boarding will now be easier on him. Maya lost a little ground on her housetraining while at the vet's office, but that was to be expected. We get back to our normal routine and I keep a vigilant eye on her to intercept any accidents in the house. I continue to accompany her while outside in order to praise her for appropriate behavior. She is becoming more comfortable in the backyard during the day, so I decide to start leaving her out by herself and watch from the window. I notice she is much more confident on the times Zippy goes out with her. She will explore the yard a little, do her business, then explore a little more until called to come in. When she is out by herself; she goes out, does her business, comes right back to the door and waits. I feel pretty good about her progress over the month since she joined our family.

CHAPTER 2

NEW YEAR'S EVE isn't much of an event at our house these days; we stay home, watch a movie, munch on snacks, watch the Times Square Celebration on TV, then go to bed. This year is no different. The dogs chew on their bones while we watch our movie and then are fast asleep on the couch when the New York Celebration starts. Neither one seems very impressed when woken up to don a Happy New Year hat and listen to Wayne and I wind the noisemakers, yelling "Happy New Year" to each other. 12:01 a.m. and we are done, ready to go to bed. The neighbors however, aren't quite done with their celebrating. The night erupts with booming fireworks from multiple locations around town. All of us startle from the suddenness of the barrage and then realize, we won't be going to bed just yet. We go to the window to watch the unsolicited show until it is over and possible to get some sleep. After a few oohs and aahs, I notice Maya is back under the living room chair, wild eyed and visibly shaking. Oh crap, she has probably never heard fireworks before and doesn't know what's going on. It has never crossed my mind that this might be traumatic for her. Zip likes to watch them and has even gone to watch firework shows with us in the past. It just never occurred to me. I bring her out from under the chair, sit her beside Zip at the window, let her see the light flashes and that Zip is unconcerned by it all. She stays beside him, but continues to shake and glance around with frantic, rolling eyes. After about half an hour, the fireworks begin to taper off. Wayne heads upstairs to bed. I wait until it has been quiet for another half an hour before I take Maya out one last time for the night. It is pretty cold out tonight, Maya is calmer but still nervous and not at all interested in wasting any time out here. I can see her nose twitching at the sulfuric odor lingering in the haze laden sky as she circles around finding her favorite spot. Right at the very moment she squats to do her business, a dud firework explodes off to our left with a ground shaking concussion. Maya yelps, jumps sideways about a foot then races back to the porch dribbling her interrupted business the whole way. She is absolutely in a panic. I scoop her up and carry her back inside. She is whimpering and quivering all over as I sit down on the couch with her. I turn off the TV, call Zippy over to help calm her down. An hour passes before she begins to show signs of calming. I am exhausted from the stress and late hour when we finally go up for bed. Zippy climbs into the dog bed, Maya follows readily. I place the blanket over both of them then get myself settled in. Before my eyes even have a chance to close, Maya is out of the bed... pacing, panting heavily and whimpering. It is now 2:30 in the morning, far later than I normally am awake. I grab my pillow and a blanket, tuck Maya back into the dog bed and lay down on the floor beside her resting my hand under her chin. Uncomfortable as I am, I think I fall asleep before she does. When I awaken again, it is five a.m., I slip back into my bed for a few more hours of sleep. Maya must be just as tired, she doesn't stir until 8:30.

Maya appears to have forgotten her fright of last night and we go about our usual New Year's Day; first watching the Rose Bowl Parade, then spending the rest of the day with family, where we partake in the traditional pork and sauerkraut dinner. After returning back home, the dogs have begun play wrestling on the living room floor while we are watching TV. Soon I find myself watching the dogs more than the TV. Glancing over at Wayne reveals he is watching them as well. For a couple of weeks now Zip has decided that grabbing Maya's ear and tugging her across the floor is great fun. Maya takes this in the spirit it is intended. Today however, she decides to give him a dose of his own medicine and grabs his back leg, tugging it out behind him. So, there they are. Zip's leg is stretched out behind him, Maya's ear, is in his mouth as they spin around in circles. Such a comical position, we can't help but laugh. This of course, eggs them both on and they kick their antics into overdrive; racing from room to room, jumping over each other, tugging on each other and wrestling.

"Who needs television, when you can just watch a pair of wiener dogs play?" I remark.

"Yeah Mom, wiener dogs playing is pretty funny tonight."

"Wienervision." I declare.

"Wienervision?"

"Wienervision is when you watch wiener dogs playing like you would watch television." I explain.

My son's response to this new word leaves me feeling like I am being humored, but it does grow on us and as we have more and more opportunity to watch wienervision, it becomes a part of our daily vocabulary.

Tomorrow is back to school and work again. Wayne has already gone to bed. I watch TV for a little while longer then take Maya outside for her final bathroom break of the day. I set her down in the yard, prepared to wait while she circles around before doing her business. After having such a good day today, I am shocked when Maya cowers down, whimpering and cringing between my legs. Apparently she has not forgotten her trauma from last night's firework fiasco. Feeling dejected over losing so much progress with her potty training, I walk about the frosted yard in my pajamas, slippers and winter coat hoping Maya will eventually do her business. She follows me step for step, whimpering and cringing the whole way. Finally after about ten minutes, she gives in and does her business. I praise her lavishly before quickly darting back inside to the blessed warmth the house provides. The next few nights see a continuation of her fearful behavior, but thankfully each night shows a decrease in the severity and by the end of the week, she is again able to go outside at night unattended.

Now that the holidays are over, there is a new puppy obedience class starting at the agility club. Maya is signed up to attend. Even though I have been working with her at home, she needs exposure to other dogs and people to learn good social skills and obedience in all situations. Thankfully Maya's class and Zip's are on the same day. Maya goes first. The puppy class is comprised of mostly larger breeds of puppies with Maya and one other dog being the only small dogs. She handles the introductions very well then basically ignores the other dogs for the rest of the class. I am pleasantly surprised at how well she focuses and responds to the commands. She seems to be enjoying herself and almost appears to be actually showing off.

We sit down and relax until the advanced obedience is over and Zip's agility group starts. Maya sits in Wayne's lap and actually watches the other dogs going through their class. While Zip and I take our turn running the agility course, I can hear her whining anxiously from the edge of the ring. Wayne manages to keep her confined to his lap throughout the entire class, but as soon as we are finished, she flies into the ring as fast as her little legs will go, straight to where Zip and I are standing. She wiggles excitedly for a second then darts over to the nearest obstacle. I manage to catch up to her in time stepping on the end of her leash keeps her from attempting to navigate the obstacle. Even though she obviously, shows an interest in agility, she is not old enough yet and still needs to master her obedience training first. Her turn at the course will come in the future, not today.

One of the other agility club members and her husband are photographers. They are setting up a day for fellow club members to have portraits done of their dogs and I schedule a session for Zip and Maya. The morning of the shoot they both get baths and a good brushing. Zip had his portrait done a couple of years ago. This time I want one of just Maya and then one of the two of them together. Zip is rather indifferent about the whole thing. Maya on the other hand, is her typical fun loving, curious self. She finds the whole event entertaining and getting her to sit still and look in a particular direction is quite a feat. The previews look like there will be some really nice pictures to choose from. When the proofs come back, I am thrilled with the results and have a tough time choosing just one of Maya by herself and just one of both dogs. Eventually, I do make up my mind. The finished portraits really capture their personalities. Zippy looking stoic and serious, while Maya has an impish glint in her eyes.

Maya is five months old now and her coat is starting to get some length to it. Her ears are losing that fluffy look and are growing long and silky. Her tail fur is also starting to lengthen. She goes through awkward stages where hair curls and sticks out in all directions. Sometimes she looks like she has devilish horns on top of her ears, a forked twig at the end of her tail and a bull's eye circle of hair on her behind. As her tail grows into a beautiful fan shape, she begins to become very protective of it. She doesn't care to have it brushed and when you try to handle it, she tucks it up under her as if, she is saying, "Leave my pretty tail alone." When there are bows in her ears, I truly do believe she knows how cute she is. Her attitude changes and she prances around willing everybody to admire her. It probably doesn't help that we are always telling her how beautiful she is. Are dogs vain? I suspect Maya may be.

The following six weeks pass quickly. Maya has

completed her puppy basic obedience class with flying colors and has her first certificate of achievement. Zip has also completed his class. Both are ready to move up a level. After a two week break, classes start up again. Maya is now old enough for her first beginner agility class. I can't wait to see how she does; after all, she has been watching how to do this for months now. She seems to know that it is her turn now, to do what she has watched Zip do. She is far more excited than she was for obedience class and I feel she is too excited and unfocused to begin. Trotting a few laps around the outside of the course helps to calm her down and regain her focus. The littlest dogs go first, with the jump heights set at only two inches off the ground. Maya sails over the jumps with ease, races through the tunnel without hesitation, noses her way through the chute without getting lost or tangled up in it. Pretty good so far. Those are the easiest obstacles. The remaining are sometimes difficult for small dogs simply because of their size. The dog walk ramp and A-frame do prove to be a challenge for Maya's little legs to climb, but she does manage to scramble up and back down both. The weave poles are confusing at first try to all dogs. Maya is no exception, she will need to practice this obstacle, until she finds the right pace and form. The last obstacle is the teeter totter. Typical of small dogs, Maya struggles with this one, as did Zip. She just doesn't have enough body weight to tip the balance until she is three quarters of the way down the obstacle. All in all, her first class goes well.

She enjoyed herself and that's what matters.

A few weeks into the new classes, Zip seems to be having trouble increasing his speed through the course for the intermediate level, so we drop him back to the level he feels comfortable with. We are not doing this for competition, this is for fun and exercise. I will not push him beyond that. Maya is doing well in her class and just having a ball. She is so amusing to watch, the joy is written all over her face for the obstacles she enjoys and the concentration is just as evident on the obstacles she struggles with. The teeter totter turns out to be her nemesis. She just hasn't gotten to the point where she knows when to shift her weight and lower it gently to the ground.

Half way through the classes I start having some health problems but I keep going about our normal routines anyway. One evening in particular, it is Zip's turn to run the course, part way through I have a sharp pain shoot from my hip and all the way down my leg. I do a kind of stutter step and slow to a walk. Zip picks up on it instantly, turning to glance back at me as he adjusts his pace to match mine. We slowly finish the course but Zip is now hesitant and unsure. I sit down until it is our turn again. We enter the ring and I give him the command to start the course. He does not respond. He sits at the start line and refuses to go. This has never happened before. We try for about ten minutes to encourage him to engage in running the course, to no avail. He mopes along beside me at times then just walks away. The trainer and I decide to sit him out for the rest of the class, give him a break and come back at it next week.

I have no residual pain or soreness the next day, or for the rest of that week. When we return for classes, Maya is first. We go for the entire hour with no problems, enjoying ourselves and learning to be more efficient navigating the course. Now it is time for Zip's class. He has spent the past hour exploring the inside of the barn where the agility course is set up. I hand Maya over to Wayne and take Zip to the course entrance. We are up first, I give Zip the "go" command, and nothing. No response at all. He just sits there, looking around the perimeter of the barn. The trainer and I exchange a frustrated look while I step off the course to let the next dog go ahead. The remainder of the hour meets with the same results. Even when the trainer tries to take Zip onto the course, he does not respond. He continues to watch the edges of the barn.

The following week the source of his distraction comes to light when, while I am taking Maya through her class, Zip gets away from Wayne, runs into the back corner of the barn and begins to bark excitedly at what turns out to be a fledgling wild bird floundering about on the floor. Just as I reach him and see what it is he is barking at, he grabs hold of the bird and quickly dispenses of it. This behavior is fairly new for Zip, it began last spring when a strong wind storm dislodged a bird nest from the eaves of our porch. There were several fledgling birds in it, Zip discovered the nest and found its contents to be irresistible. Dachshunds are a hunting breed, but they aren't supposed to be bird dogs. Badger is what they were bred to hunt, guess I forgot to tell Zippy that. Maybe since he has never encountered a badger, he decided to take advantage of what was available. Zippy thinks he is a bird dog and he turns out to be pretty good at it. Every spring, when the fledglings leave their nests, I invariably find at least one pile of feathers in the yard. Maya does not find this activity worthy of partaking in, wants nothing to do with it, whatsoever.

Zippy hones his hunting technique this spring and summer. He actually is getting quite good at catching any unsuspecting bird that lands in our yard. He will pick a spot in the center of our yard, which is completely open except for one Maple tree in the back corner and sit completely immobile until a bird lands within range. When it is not facing him, he shoots off across the yard, like a small black torpedo and actually catches the bird unaware from time to time. Having caught the bird, he decapitates it, pulls all the feathers out and then leaves the naked carcass laying in the yard for me to hit with the lawnmower, not very pleasant... especially if it has been there for a few days. Maya watches all of this from the back porch.

Not interfering in any way, not even after the bird is caught. Apparently, hunting wild birds is beneath her.

Zippy's taste of hunting at the agility barn turns out to be an insurmountable obstacle. He now has no desire to run the course, is only interested in hunting every corner for whatever critter he can find. I eventually withdraw him from the class and only take Maya. Now that the weather is getting hot, classes are later in the evening. It is still hot, humid and dusty inside the barn, so Wayne and Zip stay home for "guy time." Actually, I think both of them have gotten bored with the whole thing. Maya on the other hand, is still having fun with the class. She is getting better at most of the obstacles and looks so darn cute with her ears flouncing about when she runs and jumps. In addition to her agility training, I am working with her at home on freestyle, a choreographed dance type routine between dog and owner. We are just kind of "winging" it on this, but we are both having fun. She has learned to spin around in both directions, back-up, weave a figure eight between my legs and hop through my looped arms. I try to put a routine together to what I think is a perfect song for her, "Little Bitty Pretty One." She is such a show off. Too bad we have yet to have an opportunity to do our routine anywhere but home.

My health issues continue to be an escalating problem and unfortunately, I am forced into missing a few classes, while at the same time there are problems arising among some of the club members that eventually cause a split into two separate groups. For both of those reasons combined, I opt to discontinue our participation. It saddens me that Maya will be missing out on an activity she so enjoys. We will find other ways to keep her stimulated and engaged. We start going to as many new and interesting places as possible. Sometimes it is a state park, a playground, a pet store, a parade or even for a picnic. Everything is an adventure for Maya. She doesn't care where, when or what we do. She is truly a type A personality, giving any experience one hundred percent and loving it all.

June brings Wayne's annual week at MDA summer camp. He is excited as usual. I have learned over the past four years of his attendance to relax and enjoy this time to recharge my own batteries. This will be the first time Maya experiences "her" boy being gone for an extended period of time. The day arrives for the three hour drive to the campground; both dogs go along for the ride. I have already learned with Zippy that if he goes along, sees where Wayne is, he doesn't spend the whole week looking for him. Maya is far more bonded to Wayne than Zippy is. I hope this works for her as well. Typically Maya thinks this is another grand adventure and when we arrive at the campground, she bursts out of the car, ready for fun. While at the registration table, Maya eagerly greets every person and appears to be quite comfortable with the mass of people, wheelchairs, other medical equipment and general pandemonium. Wayne's camp volunteer helps unload the bags from the car and set everything up in his cabin. After the bed is made, we sit on the bed to say our goodbyes in private and both dogs hop up onto the bed and proceed to make themselves comfortable. I have to carry Maya out of the cabin and back to the car. She is visibly confused and reluctant to leave "her" boy out of her sight. This could be a longer week than usual.

Both dogs and I load into the car and after one final wave goodbye, we start the journey back home. Zippy settles down in the backseat without any hesitation. Maya however, seems lost in the front seat without Wayne. She whines, pants, rolls her eyes and will not settle down. She begins to climb over the center console, jump into the backseat, down onto the floor, and then back up to the front seat. This proves to be such a distraction that I miss the exit onto the road that takes us east toward home. Continuing on north to find a place to turn around is further than I would have anticipated. The next thing I know, I am driving across the grated metal bridge over the Ohio River, when suddenly Maya escalates into a full blown panic attack right beside me in the front passenger seat. Distraught over my inability to both drive the car safely and address her obvious distress, I thankfully soon come to an exit on the other side of the bridge where I pull off at the first available spot to assess her condition. Her eyes are glassy and rolling wildly, she is panting and salivating heavily, her sides are heaving, she is trembling uncontrollably and has gotten sick all over the floor in the back. Years ago when I had taken one of my yellow labs through obedience training, I had witnessed another dog have a panic attack. Maya's condition now looks just like that dog did. It does not look good and I am worried.

I quickly lift her out of the car, grab hold of Zip's leash and head over to a shaded grassy spot. I sit down cradling her in my lap trying to calm her down and cool her off. Thinking back to the dog that had a panic attack during obedience training, I recall the trainer first, gently poured cool water over the dog and when that did not help, she carried the dog into the swimming pool where she held it only partially submerged in the water until it started to cool off and calm down. I dash back to the car, grab some napkins and my bottle of water, dash back to the shady area; sit back down with Maya in my lap. I wet the napkins with the water and then hold them against her belly. While keeping the napkins wet, I move them from her belly to her chest and then under her armpit area, talking to her soothingly the entire time. Zip sits right beside us, watching her intently, occasionally giving her a quick lick on her muzzle. Thirty minutes of this passes before I really see a significant improvement. Her eyes begin to come back into focus and her breathing slows down. She is still trembling when she tentatively steps off my lap into the grass and begins to hesitantly walk around. Zip matches her every step, as if they are attached at the shoulders. Another fifteen minutes, she is calm enough to relieve herself and take a few laps of water. I don't want to let her drink too much, we still have to cross that same bridge to get back on the road home and I have no idea how to manage it. Before getting back on the road, I put the dogs in the car with the air conditioning on, walk across the grassy area to a gas station to inquire if there is a different way to get back onto the correct road without crossing that same bridge. Sadly, the attendant informs me, there is no other way to go without adding excessive miles to the trip and having to cross a different bridge of the same design.

Now what? I sit in the car for a few minutes thinking how am I going to accomplish this? My only solution, for better or worse, is to have Zip in the front passenger seat and lay Maya across my lap while I drive across the bridge. Hoping that the body contact and Zip's presence will keep her calmer. As we approach the bridge, I feel myself tense and try deep breathing, forcing myself to relax as much as possible. Luckily, it is not a long bridge. There is some minor panting, whining and eye rolling from Maya. I talk to her,

"It's okay Maya. We're almost across it. Don't have another melt-down. You'll be alright."

Shortly after we have crossed the hateful bridge, she starts to calm down again, stops trembling and eventually climbs over into the seat with Zip. Success, the rest of the trip home is uneventful. Both dogs have fallen asleep, not waking until we pull up in front of the house. My tremendous sense of absolute relief gets the better of me and once inside the house, I collapse on the couch.

I have made no plans for this week. I do what I want, when I want. I don't cook, go to bed when I am tired and wake up when I wake up. Selfish, yes in a way it is, however this is the only time I will have for the next year; I have to make it count. Both dogs seem to enjoy the quiet relaxed atmosphere. We go hang out at different parks in the morning, nap on the couch during the heat of the day and then go for a walk every evening before watching some kind of "chick flick" movie until bedtime.

Of course, the week is over before I know it and it is time to bring our "boy" back home. After the last car ride, I am now forewarned to Maya's potential for panic attacks in the car. I leave the house forearmed as well; the training crate is placed in the back seat, Maya safely encased, with a direct view of Zippy calmly enjoying the ride. Much easier, and we reach the campground in what seems like no time at all. Wayne is busy saying his goodbyes and giving out final hugs as I get the dogs out of the car. Maya immediately picks up on where he is and is straining at her leash practically screaming in excitement. Wayne is sitting on the grass and as Maya closes in on him, I drop her leash watching in amusement as she launches herself into his lap and engages in the most enthusiastic "kissy wiggle" we have ever seen. If she had a thought bubble over her head, I could easily imagine it would read, "my boy, my boy, I missed you. My boy, my boy, I'm so happy we found you!" Her greeting is so enthusiastic he falls over backward, laughing as now both dogs are climbing all over him kissing and nuzzling every inch of him drawing attention from everyone nearby. Maya's joy and relief are perfectly evident in her expression. After a couple of minutes, she does calm down, but will not leave his lap willingly and as we load his gear into the trunk of the car, she is never more than a few inches from his side.

MDA Summer Camp is officially over for this year. Having stowed all of Wayne's gear, we open the car doors, Zip hops into the back seat readily but as Wayne prepares to settle in to the front passenger seat, Maya beats him to it. She is more than ready to assume her usual position on his lap for the ride home. After her panic attack, I am hesitant to allow this, but decide to give it a try. If she does begin to panic, there are now two of us to deal with it in a much safer manner and can pull over and put her back into the crate if needed.

Wayne is very chatty at first, giving me a quick review of his week, but then he falls asleep for the majority of the ride home. Maya lies on the seat beside him with her chin on his lap and also falls asleep. A quick glance in the backseat reveals that Zip is also sound asleep. This will be my last bit of silence for a while. Once Wayne is rested up, the next few days will be a minute by minute replay of every moment at camp. This week is good for all of us, but I am glad it is only a week; I probably couldn't stand any longer than that. As I glance over at Maya, still sleeping with her chin on his lap, I don't know if she could stand any more either.

4th of July is now upon us and I have not forgotten the New Year's Eve fireworks episode. If the fourth were just a one day holiday in our area, I could plan to put some distance between Maya and the upsetting noise. Unfortunately, the fourth is a week-long celebration for some of our fellow residents. I guess my only option is to take advantage of this and try to desensitize her now, while she is young. The first crackles break the evening wind-down soon enough and not surprisingly, Maya startles and begins to roll her eyes. My plan of attack is to begin by distracting her and making the noise a signal for something good. Armed with a pocket full of treats and a squeaky toy, I sit down on the floor and start playing tug with Zip, counting on Maya's playfulness and jealousy to overcome her fear. It doesn't take long at all before she grabs hold of the toy as well and we play three way tug, while firecrackers explode outside. Her eyes dart in the direction of the noise but she continues to play with fervor. When the two dogs are tired of tug and drop the toy, I am ready with treats. I simply hold one in each closed hand, wait for both dogs to pick up the scent, locate the source and give me their full attention. At the next explosion I pop open my hands revealing the treats, which quickly disappear. Since Maya is calm enough to eat, my next step is load up her "treat ball" for her to roll around until a treat falls out. Works like a charm; she rolls the ball around until it is empty and has ignored the noise outside. After all that activity, she is pretty tired and stretches out beside me on the couch for a nap. One last episode with the firecrackers, Maya raises her head up briefly, then lies back down and falls asleep with no visible sign of concern.

We continue in the same manner for the rest of the week changing the games and distractions to keep her more interested in playing than in being fearful. The evening of the fourth we have a small package of fireworks from the department store to set off ourselves. Wayne and Zip normally sit on the porch to watch the "show," this year is no exception. Maya follows us outside, waits on the porch, watching while I set up our small selection. The "show" starts with one small but flashy firecracker to assess Maya's reaction. She has her tail tucked and is rolling her eyes a bit, but not too bad. She isn't trying to run or hide. I decide not to let her escalate beyond this mild reaction by putting her inside only closing the storm door, which is the full glass type, so she can still see outside but have a barrier between her and the sounds and smells occurring outside. A few more small fireworks later, I see Maya sitting at the door watching without any apparent signs of distress. We are half way through the package. Now I start on the bigger fireworks. Zip is watching every burst with his usual relaxed interest and I can't help but wonder if he agrees with each of Wayne's critiques. I have left the biggest of the fireworks for last. The showering fountain will be our grand finale. Maya has begun scratching at the door to come out. I let her out and set her on Wayne's lap before lighting the end of our show. We dutifully ooh and aah at the colorful shower of sparks erupting in the night sky. Maya has tolerated the fireworks pretty well. I doubt that she enjoyed the event but, her desire to be with her family overcame her fears. I count that as progress.

Our fireworks show is over early everybody else will be starting soon and I know when not to push any further. I clean up our debris and take Maya out to potty before we settle in to watch TV until the neighborhood percussion symphony is over. The treat ball is full and ready for the first boom to shatter the evening's calm. It isn't long before the night erupts. I toss the treat ball onto the floor immediately and watch as Maya intently rolls it around until emptied, then a few minutes more; just to make sure it is indeed empty. Even though there are now multiple locations surrounding us setting off rocket type fireworks; Maya lies on the couch beside me, still a bit uneasy and looking up with each explosion, after about fifteen minutes, she falls asleep.

CHAPTER 3

TODAY IS MAYA'S first birthday. Her special treat will be a shopping trip to the pet store and since it is Saturday, we will make a family day of it by having a cook-out at one of our favorite state parks as well. I gather up the supplies needed for the cook-out and then we all pile into the car for the drive to the pet store. Both dogs heartily enjoy shopping for their own toys, choosing very different items. Maya's selection today is a small tennis ball with a fuzzy tail attached to it and some pupcorn treats. Zippy opts for a plush duck squeaky toy and a package of pig ears. Each dog "carries" its new toy up the aisle to the cash registers drawing plenty of attention from other shoppers. Before checking out, I pick out two frosted dog donuts to serve in lieu of a birthday cake. Back in the car and heading down the highway, I hear the unmistakable sound of a rustling plastic shopping bag. Wayne looks into the back seat and relays that both dogs have gotten their toys out of the bag and are laying on the backseat playing. They seem content for the moment, but I know they tend to get possessive with food items and that it won't be long before one of them starts rooting in the bag again. I tell Wayne to bring the bag up to the front seat and out of their reach until we return home.

The state park is not too crowded today, even though it is a beautiful late summer's day. Both dogs know this park well and our routine when visiting here. First we choose a picnic table and grill, then we unload the supplies from the car. Next the charcoal is piled up on the grill and lit. The aroma is a familiar one to the dogs and keeps their interest focused on our area. While the burgers are cooking, I set up the rest of the meal and Wayne walks the dogs around the immediate picnic site. Just when the aroma has built our appetites to stomach growling heights, the burgers are done to satisfaction. Four plates are prepared; each dog is given a small plate on the ground as Wayne and I settle in at the picnic table. Once we are all sufficiently stuffed, we clean up our area and pack the supplies back into the car. Now we are ready to explore the park grounds. The dogs are anxious to get going and turn toward the bridge that leads down to the river.

We spend about an hour climbing around on the rocks, watching the waterfall, and hiking up stream to calmer water so the dogs can stand at the edge of the water and cool off. Neither dog has ever shown any interest in actually swimming; wading is about as far as these two wiener dogs will go. I suspect that dachshunds, given their body structure, short stubby legs, long torso and pencil thin tails, probably aren't very good at swimming in general. On the way back to the bridge, we come across a small pooled area among the rocks full of little fish. The dogs are instantly interested. Zippy wades into the pool up to his belly and tries to catch the fish while Maya paces around the perimeter whining excitedly. We let the dogs' fish for a few minutes, then coax them away from the pool while no fish have been harmed. Back up the path, across the bridge and back to the car. Both dogs then sleep in the backseat all the way home.

The final part of Maya's birthday celebration comes after supper. She is given her doggie donut for dessert. Of course, Zippy gets one too and they both begin by licking the frosting off the top of the donut. Once that is done, they each try to bite into the donut but decide it is too large and sit staring at me to do something about the situation. They don't realize that the donuts crumble pretty easily, so I break each one into smaller pieces easier for them to manage and in short order both donuts are completely gone. Happy first Birthday Maya.

The next day, I decide to try out the leash coupler I found at the pet store. This item is supposed to prevent the dog's leashes from tangling, while on a walk by connecting two dogs to one leash. In theory, it sounds like a good idea. From the first step out the door the dogs know something is different and so do I. The first thing I notice is that there is no pulling on the leash that I am holding. That's great for me but apparently, not for the dogs. Rather than pulling against the leash, they are pulling against each other. Maya typically weaves from side to side on a walk, while Zip is a dog on a mission looking straight ahead the whole time. With the coupler, when Maya darts off to the side, she pulls Zippy with her and when Zip forges dead ahead, he drags Maya with him. I am hopeful at this point, that as we continue on our walk the dogs will figure out that they have to work together in order to make progress forward comfortable. On the return home, it seems like they are getting the hang of it but then Maya makes another attempt to weave to the left. That's it... Zip has had enough of this. He sits down in the middle of the street and refuses to move another inch. Maya keeps trying to move forward. Nope, no way, he will not budge. He is in full protest. Luckily we are almost home, so I unclip Maya and carry her the rest of the way home. Letting Zip have the leash to himself, which is just fine with him. So, my lesson for today, what sounds good in theory, doesn't always pan out in practice. I do try the coupler again and again over the next few weeks, but then with no change in the dog's acceptance of it, put it away for good; it just is not practical for us.

Now that Maya is a year old, we can see she has a very distinct personality. She is the princess and we are all to treat her as such. She remains fun loving, curious and always eager for a new experience or adventure. Zippy let's her have her own way most of the time. When he puts his paw down however, his word is the law and Maya respects it. She is also bold and confident when Zip is with her. On her own; she is more cautious and looks to her humans for direction. Her coat is coming in really nice now, gaining length and remaining silky and glossy. We have noticed an amusing habit with the two dogs, they have begun doing everything in tandem... sit, down, stand, bark, eat, sleep, turn their heads. They are two peas in a pod. When they are sleeping, some part of them is always touching the other one. I can't believe how much enjoyment comes with owning a pair of small house dogs. I don't think I'll ever have a single dog again. It seems a shame now to deprive a dog of the daily companionship they instinctively need. Maya has brought out the goofball in Zip that had been missing for the past few years. He just seems more at ease now. He no longer gets upset when we leave the house without him and he is eating much better than he used to. He has actually put on enough weight that his ribs and hip bones are no longer visible.

Since Maya has come into her own confidence, she is becoming rather sassy at times. One area in particular, could get her into more trouble than she can handle at a mere 11 pounds. The neighbors on either side of us had each gotten littermate black lab/shepherd mix pups that are now full grown and weighing in at a hundred pounds each. These guys are both friendly, sociable dogs who frequently trot past our house to visit each other; sometimes stopping in our front yard to leave their mark. Both Zip and Maya are not too thrilled about this and whenever they view this routine, are pretty vocal in their protest. If we happen to have our dogs outside on the porch, front yard or driveway and either of these dogs trots by, Zip and Maya will explode like two bullets from a gun barrel to remove the offending dog from their space. Zip is content to see them off his property. Maya however, does not stop until they are across the street and back into their own yards. At first, we all find it amusing to watch both of these 100 pound dogs run from an 11 pound ball of furry fury with their tails tucked firmly between their legs. Each time the neighbor dogs are intimidated back home, Maya becomes bolder, barking more insistently and pushing them further into their yards, before turning around and returning home. A few of these episodes is all it takes to realize the potential dangers of allowing this to continue. The neighbor's work on keeping their dogs from roaming and I re-emphasize the voice commands of "leave it" and "wait". Thankfully everybody learned their lesson before anyone got hurt. Zip and Maya have both neighbor dogs so intimidated; all it takes is a few barks to send them both back to their respective homes now. They seem to realize there is no need for chasing anymore and that it won't be tolerated anyway.

Just a few weeks before Christmas, we are over for Sunday dinner. Dad and I leave for a few hours. Wayne and both dogs stay behind with grandma. When we return to the house it is already dark, as we enter the door and are greeted by all the dogs and one kid scrambling for attention, Maya's paw gets stepped on. We have no idea, in the pandemonium, if it was a person or another dog. Regardless, she lets out a terrible yelp of pain, instantly holding the paw up and refusing to put weight on it. I scoop her up and examine the paw. There is no obvious damage. She doesn't flinch or yelp when I flex the paw or leg and the toes do not evoke a response either. It's just a slight bruise I think, she'll be fine by morning at the latest.

The rest of that evening, she refuses to bear weight on that paw and we lift her onto the couch and then back down, as well as carrying her up and down the steps. At bedtime, she settles into the dog bed with Zip and they are both sound asleep quickly. I breathe a sigh of relief, believing that she'll be fine in the morning and I can drop Wayne off at school, go do the last of my Christmas shopping and have the gifts, either hidden or wrapped before it's time for school to let out.

Morning arrives all too quickly with the startling jolt of the alarm clock going off. After a few slaps at the snooze button, I resign myself to getting up to a cold December morning and getting on with the day. The dogs are not too eager to get up before daylight either and need to be called out of their bed. Honestly, I don't give Maya's paw more than a passing thought, until she takes one step out of the dog bed, screams horribly and then crumples over onto the floor continuing to scream in obvious pain. Oh God no, I think to myself. She really is hurt. I feel terrible letting her suffer through the night with an injury, apparently far worse than I had realized. I worry there might be something broken. Leaving Zip at home, I drop Wayne off at school and take her straight to the vet's office.

In the exam room, I explain to Dr. Kendrick the circumstances of the previous evening's injury to her right front paw in careful detail. When I finish, the doctor smiles at me kindly and asks,

"You're certain; it is her right front paw?"

"Yes, the right one. She won't use it at all." I reply, still worried for my little one.

"Well, if it is her right paw" he explains, "I have to wonder now, why, she is holding up her left paw."

As his words sink through my guilt laden worry, dumbfounded I glance down and sure enough, Maya is sitting on the exam table, holding up her left paw and looking expectantly at the doctor whose smile has grown into a grin and is now accompanied by a chuckle.

"You're kidding me; all of this has been an act?" I question in disbelief.

"Sure looks that way, but I'll check both of her paws thoroughly, to make absolutely certain." answers the vet, still with the grin spread kindly across his face.

Maya never so much as flinches while both of her paws are carefully examined and I am still trying to understand how this little pup so convincingly manipulated me. Dr. Kendrick, apparently picks up on my chagrin and explains,

"Small house dogs can be very good at exaggerating an injury. Many other people have been fooled just like you have. Both of her front paws are perfectly fine. She is a wonderfully healthy, albeit dramatic, little girl. Take her home, go about your normal routine and don't worry about her right paw or her left one either. She most likely will walk out of here just fine."

"I was going to go to the pet store today and do their Christmas shopping. I guess she can pick out her own gift. That should be a pretty good reward for her performance." I now laughingly, reply.

Dr. Kendrick laughs, shakes his head, giving me a pat on the shoulder, while saying,

"That's the spirit."

"Let's hope there is not an encore performance."

After I settle up for the office visit, Maya prances out the door, using all four paws equally and just, oh so proud of herself. All the way to the pet store, I continue to shake my head in disbelief. The quality of her performance was top notch, worthy of an Oscar. Oh well, another lesson learned, time to let it go and get on with the day. At the pet store, Maya enjoys herself immensely picking out a new tennis ball with furry tail and playing with it in the aisle in absolute joy. Many other customers stop to watch her antics commenting on how cute she is. If they only knew that she is actually the dog version of a triple threat; cute, playful, and quite the actress.

I do manage to finish the Christmas shopping and place the purchases in the trunk of the car so Maya can begin to forget about the new toy she picked out. Once back at home, the gifts are hidden and we go about the rest of the day without incident. I continue to be suspicious over Maya's performance for the next few days but, thankfully there is no encore. Her paw is fine and she has returned to her normal activities, seeming to have forgotten about the injury completely.

Christmas arrives, and both dogs open their gifts with gusto. Ripping, shaking and tearing at the present until it is unwrapped then playing with each toy for a few minutes before settling down to chew on their new bones. For some reason unknown to me, they have recently begun a new routine with new toys and bones. They may have the exact same item given at the exact same time when one or the other dog will stop playing with their item and sit, staring at the other one who continues to play with their item completely ignoring the stare. After a while the one playing will abandon the item, which is quickly snatched up by the previously staring dog. Now the roles are reversed, the one who lost the item becomes the one to sit and stare. I don't get it, no matter how many bones or toys there are, somebody sits and stares as if they are the most deprived dog on the planet. They seem to have some sort of agreement between them for the rules to this game. Patience and focus are apparently very important factors.

This winter turns out to bring a rather heavy amount of snow to deal with. Zippy lost his enthusiasm for plunging through deep snowfall a few years ago. Maya however, still thinks this is a novelty. She continues to pounce around in the backyard collecting snowballs on her fur until she can barely walk from the weight and restricted range of motion. Upon returning inside, she has now improved her snowball removal technique to include, bending her head way under her chest and between her front legs to pull snowballs off her chest and belly. The top of her head rests on the floor; her ears fan out on the floor. She looks like she is trying to stand on her head.

As the snowfall continues to mount, I begin to shovel a path for the dogs to have an easier time navigating during potty breaks. Zippy uses the path faithfully, never deviating from it, returning as quickly as possible back to the porch where he watches Maya insistently attempt to plow through the drifts and piled up snow. While the snow remains on the ground Maya persists with this behavior, to the point that she now has an iced over slide formed at the end of the shoveled path which, she scrambles up and then slides back down every time she is out in the yard. She seems to be taking great joy in this activity and appears quite proud of herself, eyes glinting, tail wagging and tongue hanging out the side of her mouth.

The days have begun to warm up enough to melt the snow somewhat and yet the nights are still below the freezing point, causing an icy crust to form on top of the snow pack. When this crust is strong enough to hold his weight, Zippy begins to venture out on to it, gingerly picking his way about the yard making sure all is still in order in his domain. Having company around the entire yard again gives Maya so much pleasure that she romps and dances about, often sliding into Zip, knocking them both off their feet causing a mad scramble to right themselves and get on with their business.

Winter's icy grip is loosening. The first refrains of spring's heralding are tuning up. Patches of sun warmed grass are widening daily. Green tips of daffodils are poking through their blankets of snow and the birds have returned to pick out their nesting sites. While Zippy turns his gaze upward to watch the increasing activity in the skies, Maya is finding many new treasures in the yard, sticks broken off the maple tree, gravel thrown up by the snowplow and little pieces of paper blown in by the harsh winds. Everything she finds is given her full attention, either to be carried about proudly, to be chewed on or stored in a pile near the bottom of the porch steps.

When the snow has melted completely, the yard becomes a muddy mess and the dogs begin to leave a trail of muddy paw prints from the back door through the kitchen and into either, the dining room or the front room. I don't mind mopping the floors, but three or four times a day, is just more than I care to do, so an old towel is kept by the back door and every time the dogs re-enter the house, they wait on an area rug until their paws and bellies are wiped off. They have learned this routine pretty well and once the towel is brought out, they will wait on the rug without a command, actually needing a command to leave the rug when wiping the paws is no longer necessary.

My sister, her husband and their 5 kids are coming for the Easter Holiday and will be staying with us for a couple of days. This will be Maya's first exposure to the whole family in her home. I have no idea how she will react but am curious to see how tolerant she will be. I know that Zippy loves all kids. Hopefully Maya will follow his example.

From the moment they arrive, the excited energy surrounding the kids is just too much for Maya to practice restraint around. She seems to find them to be unpredictable and is startled every time somebody moves. When there are nine people in the house, somebody is always moving and Maya barks sharply with each movement large or small. If someone goes upstairs, when they come back down Maya responds with a volley of alarm barking, as if she forgot they had gone upstairs. The kids find this amusing at first but, by the second day are as tired of it as I am. The youngest of my sister's children is the biggest animal lover of the group and she tries patiently to make "friends" with Maya who alternates between nervous uncertainty and curious interest. They do come to an unspoken understanding of how much space to give each other and Maya begins to engage in cautious play and does come to snuggle up against her leg when the kids have settled down to watch television.

When the kids beg to take the dogs for a walk, I leash them both up, hand them over to the kids and watch as both dogs refuse to walk... looking back over their shoulders wondering why "mom" isn't coming along. The kids try and try to no avail, to encourage the dogs to walk down the road with them. I decide to give them a helping hand and join them for their walk. Now the dogs are happy as can be to trot down the road with their "pack" of people. We all walk to the ball field and playground where kids and dogs alike run around the field and play on the swings and slide. The kids think it is the funniest thing to watch the dogs go down the sliding board and sit on my lap at the swings. Having sufficiently tired the kids out, we head back up to the house where it is time for them to load up the van and head back home to Pennsylvania. The kids start giving us our goodbye hugs, the youngest, includes both dogs in her round of hugs and earns a slight lick on the cheek from Maya, which elicits an ear to ear grin and a return kiss to Maya's nose. They have apparently, formed a tentative bond after all.

The next few months are full of the normal chores and activities that come with the summer season leaving no shortage of entertainment options for dogs and humans alike. Every activity I partake in around the house is apparently of great interest to the dogs. They watch all my movements waiting for the opportunity to jump in and provide their own type of assistance. This usually is not actually valuable assistance, but does sometimes prove to be comic relief.

One particular morning during early fall, I stop in at town hall before heading to a doctor appointment. While there, the Mayor and one of the town's employees call me over to the town's garage, showing me a young cat and seven kittens in a cardboard box. It turns out, while out doing maintenance the guys found the whole brood huddled together in the cardboard box, which was in a ditch along the side of the road. Some people can be so cruel... how do they expect a most likely by the looks of her, a first time mother to care for that many kittens? By scrounging for food? Feral and free roaming cats are a huge community issue in our area. There seems to be a cultural acceptance that spaying and neutering of pets but, cats especially, is an unnecessary expense and that cats are disposable, easily replaced by the next cute little kitten that comes along. Entire neighborhoods are often over run with cats; leading to property damage, decreased home values and at times, over-powering odors of cat urine permeating yards and community spaces. Sand boxes do not exist at playgrounds, it is common knowledge any sandbox would quickly become the community litter box. The animal shelter and humane society for our area are so overwhelmed with cats and kittens, they will only occasionally accept more. Sometimes they only take them long enough to euthanize them.

The guys have told me that the humane society has agreed to come tomorrow morning and pick up the mother cat and kittens, but will have to euthanize them all. Their facility is full. While we are talking, the momma cat is rubbing against my legs and purring. I reach down to pet her and am instantly shocked at how thin she is. She is a dark gray tabby and is social and affectionate, definitely used to people. Six of the kittens are black and white and look to be about four weeks old. They are frisky and also show no fear around us. The seventh kitten is the same dark gray tabby coloring as the momma cat. He is significantly smaller than the other kittens and upon picking it up, I see that the umbilical cord has not yet fallen off this kitten. The guys say that all of the kittens are nursing off of the momma, but that the older ones are also eating the bologna that they found in the garage fridge and put down for the momma cat. We commiserate for a few minutes on how unfair and cruel it is that all of these cats are in this situation because of people.

As I go about my errands and doctor appointment, I cannot get those cats off my mind. I am certain, the simple fact that six of the kittens are black and white, like my Cricket was, probably has a lot to do with it. By early afternoon, I realize I cannot turn my back and let any of these kitties go to the fate laid out for them. I stop back by town hall, telling the clerk to call animal control back and tell them that someone has agreed to foster the cats and when old enough, find them new homes. I can't believe I am actually about to bring eight cats into my home.

After picking Wayne up at school, we stop by the grocery store to purchase cat food and litter then stop at the local vet's office and pick up milk replacement and a kitten bottle for the smallest kitten. We then make a quick stop at the house to set up a space for the cats in the spare bedroom, get the cat carrier out of the attic and let the dogs out to potty. I know Zippy will be great with the cats, but Maya has not had any experience with cats in her home and I am not sure how she will react. Another unknown is if the cats have been socialized to dogs in their previous environment.

When we go back down to the town garage the guys are there waiting. The first comment from them is,

"Are you sure you want to do this?"

"I've thought about it since I left here this morning, and yes, I'll keep them until they are ready for new homes and you both better help with that part."

"You'll end up keeping them all." they snicker together.

"No, I will not. I like cats, you know that, but I had 17 years of cleaning a litter box and I really don't want that chore for another 17."

They elbow each other and then agree to help find homes for which ever I decide not to keep. We load all 8 cats into the carrier, toss the cardboard box they were found in into the dumpster and put the carrier into the car. During the short ride back to the house, Wayne is jabbering a mile a minute, with question after question so fast, there is not time to even answer one piece of the barrage.

Back at the house, I place the carrier on the porch directly in front of the storm door, giving the dogs on one side and the cats on the other the chance to first smell and view each other with a barrier between them. All parties are curious and show no signs of distress, so I then move the carrier inside the house. The dogs come up to sniff at the door to the carrier with caution. Momma cat responds in kind. A few minutes of checking each other out and Zippy starts to get playful, pouncing and barking at the carrier. Momma cat is not impressed and issues a warning hiss. Zip gets the hint quickly and takes a few steps back before sitting down to calmly observe the carriers occupants. Maya takes her cue from Zippy and calmly sits beside him, waiting expectantly for whatever comes next.

Momma cat has been through quite an ordeal recently. I am surprised at how calm she remains, but she sure deserves a chance to get comfortable and relax. We place the carrier on the floor in the spare bedroom, taking the door completely off and blocking the room's doorway with the baby gate. The dogs have watched all of this intently and after Wayne and I step back to let the cats settle in, both dogs assume positions that will become their norm for the next few weeks... lying in the hallway with noses pressed against the baby gate. Wayne quickly coins this activity as watching "kitty-vision." So now our entertainment options include the three ring circus of kittens playing, dogs watching "kitty-vision" and humans watching "wiener-vision."

The older kittens are quick to explore the entire room and waste no time in finding things to play with. Some of them are not appropriate and I realize how much kitten proofing needs to be done. While making the room safer for the curious kittens, I observe that even though the older kittens are eating the cat food I have set out, they continue to nurse off the momma and appear to be pushing the littlest kitten out of the way. It is going to be vital for him to get supplemental milk as quickly as possible. After mixing up the formula and filling the kitten bottle, I sit on the bedroom floor and try to get him to take the bottle; he resists the unfamiliar feeling at first but then does start to swallow small amounts of the formula. His little tummy has filled out a bit and I put him back with momma cat where he suckles a little more while momma grooms him.

I give the little guy more formula every couple of hours for the rest of the evening and he really seems to be getting the hang of the bottle. Momma cat also gets some of the formula in a bowl. She is so thin and has practically no development to her milk glands; she needs all the extra calories she can get right now. Our first day with the cats has gone well and the ensuing night also proves to be quiet and restful.

The next morning as I put more food down for momma and the older kittens; I notice the little guy is pushed far back in the carrier and feels a little cool to the touch. He does stir and utters a small mew as I rub him gently. Momma comes over, sniffs him and then walks away. This doesn't seem quite right, so I encourage her to lie in the carrier for him to nurse. Which she does as long as I stay there blocking her exit from the carrier. Satisfied that he at least has food in his belly, I put a small towel in the carrier with him for warmth and get on with the weekday morning's activities. After Wayne is delivered to school for the day, I check on the kitten again and feed him from the bottle. He is still in the same condition as earlier this morning. There may even be a trace of nasal discharge; it is too slight to be certain. I'll mow the lawn as planned then check on him again.

Two hours later when I come back in from mowing, I am shocked at how quickly the little guy has gone downhill. I am very concerned now; he is cold and unresponsive, there is now a definite discharge around his nose and when I pick him up, I can hear congestion in his breathing. As I wrap him in the towel and hold him close, he begins to stir weakly. I am not sure he will make it for the twenty minute trip to our usual veterinarian's office and he certainly needs medical attention if he is to have a chance. I decide to take him to the vet in our town even though I have not dealt with her before. Five minutes later, walking in to the reception area with the little guy wrapped in the towel, the vet pokes her head around the corner and asks if she can help, explaining that it is lunchtime and she is the only one there at the moment.

"I have a very tiny kitten here, who may be trying to die on me." I reply quickly.

The doctor scoops the bundle from my arms and whisks him back to an exam room asking me questions as she goes. Answering her barrage, I relate the circumstances of how the kitten came to be in this condition.

"He is actively dying right now. I don't know if he can turn around at this point. He at least has an upper respiratory infection, if not pneumonia and is less than a week old. That's a lot to deal with and he just may not be strong enough to fight It." she informs me.

We agree to do what can be done and hope for the best. When I try to pay for the visit, the doctor waves me off saying, "If he makes it to tomorrow, bring him back in along with the other kittens and the momma cat. I'll check them all out then we'll settle up."

Following the doctor's orders, I keep the kitten wrapped in the towel with a heating pad on low underneath him, rubbing him firmly to keep his circulation stimulated. She has also instructed that he and the momma cat be separated from the older kittens so she will devote all of her resources to him only. I sit on the couch for over an hour rubbing him constantly when I realize, I have to pee. Since Maya has laid by my leg for the entire past hour unmoving and watching the kitten with great intent, I lay the kitten beside her and watch her gently curl herself around the kitten and begin licking his face and softly nudging his chest. They'll be fine, long enough for me to run upstairs to the bathroom. Returning to the couch, Maya is still caring for the little kitten as if he is now her baby. It is wonderful to see her nurturing side since she is the one typically being babied. Another half hour of rubbing the kitten and it is time to go pick Wayne up from school. Now what? Every time I have tried to stop rubbing the kitten, he has started to stiffen up. I don't think he can be left unstimulated, but I certainly can't drive while holding and rubbing him. I settle on putting him with Maya on the front passenger seat where she can keep him warm and yet, I can reach over easily to continue rubbing him during the short six or seven minute drive to the school. Once school lets out, Wayne holds the kitten and rubs him while I explain on the way home, the events of the afternoon.

"Is he going to die, Mom?" Wayne asks softly.

"There is a good chance he will die son, but we'll keep trying to help him as much as we can."

Another hour and a half of sitting on the couch rubbing the kitten constantly and getting a few drops of formula in him from the bottle and it is time to start supper. I realize the only thing keeping this little guy alive is the constant stimulation and that we cannot continue to do this indefinitely. Not quite ready to give up on him yet, I call Wayne downstairs to take over the kitten's care while I make supper. Quick checks every few minutes, show that Wayne is doing all he can with the rubbing. Half way through supper preparations he calls out,

"Mom, the kitten is making some strange noises."

I rush in and sure enough, there is a rattily, raspy sound to his breathing far too loud for such a tiny body.

"Take him Mom, I don't want him to die in my lap." cries Wayne, in a slightly panicked voice.

I take the kitten from him. Laying it on the couch I say,

"I think his time is done. Let's just sit here and pet him until he is gone, then he will at least go knowing somebody cared about him."

Zippy and Maya both sense something is going on and join us on the couch, simply laying, watching the kitten for the next couple of minutes until, he just doesn't take another breath. I look over to Wayne,

"I think that's it. His fight is over."

"He's dead? Are you sure?

"Yeah, he's gone. He's not breathing anymore."

I turn off the heating pad. Fold the towel around him. Zip and Maya look from the kitten to me and back again, expectantly. When I don't respond, Maya begins nudging at the towel wrapped kitten, seemingly trying one last time to wake him up. I find a little box to place him in and after a somber supper, we bury the little guy in the front garden.

Later that evening while watching television, Wayne asks me if the other kittens are going to die too.

"I don't think so honey. They are much bigger and don't show any signs of being sick, but I'll take them to the vet tomorrow and make sure they are healthy.

"Good, I don't like it when they die." he responds.

After Wayne has gone to bed, I am surprised to see Momma cat tiptoeing silently down the steps. I just lay on the couch watching her investigate the downstairs area, room by room. Is she looking for the kitten, learning her new environment or both? She winds up in the living room and after a quick sniff to Zippy under his cover in the dog bed and Maya and I lying on the couch, she jumps up onto a chair where she catches a relaxing catnap. Zippy has not moved in his bed, I'm not sure that he is aware of the cat's presence downstairs. Maya however, has watched her every step, but other than a quick glance at me, shows no concern at all. When the dogs and I make our way upstairs for the night, she follows along, jumps up and climbs over the baby gate to settle down in the spare bedroom with the remaining kittens.

Last night's behavior from Momma cat shows me that she is very familiar with being inside a house. Nothing so far has startled her and she seems to know her way around a house quite well; choosing to lay on the bed and chairs, climbing up and down the stairs, looking out the windows and showing no interest in trying to go out the door when it is open. The kitchen appears to be a room she is very comfortable with. During meal preparation, she sits in the middle of the floor watching the activity, not begging or jumping onto the counters or table... just watching and waiting. Sadly my initial impression that this was someone's house cat, dumped carelessly in a ditch to fend for herself and at least one kitten, seems to be more accurate than ever.

After the school day has started, I load Momma cat and the remaining kittens back into the carrier for the promised visit to the vet. Once there, the doctor escorts us into an exam area where we are joined by several of her staff. I relate that the tiny kitten hung on for several hours before passing away just before suppertime. The vet is surprised that he made it that long. Apparently she has already shared the circumstances of the cats with her staff and they all help with the examination of the kittens. Who are declared to be six weeks old and Momma cat still a kitten herself at only eight or nine months old. Other than having some fleas, they are all fairly healthy considering what they have been through. Momma needs continued extra food to regain her body weight. All the cats are given their shots and a dose of worm medicine with a follow up dose to be administered at home along with flea treatment with spray I already have at home for use on the dogs. We all come to the consensus that the tiny kitten was born to Momma and that the remaining six were most likely from another cat. Probably they were dumped off together and the kittens began to nurse from Momma in order to survive. The great unanswerable question is if Momma had her sole kitten before or after being dumped and if anybody even knew she was pregnant. That poor little tiny kitten really never had a chance. It was just too cold at night for a days old kitten to be outside in the elements.

Each kitten, as well as Momma, get their own health record and as we begin to fill them out, it gets difficult to come up with six different ways to identify them based solely on physical characteristics as they are all similarly marked. There are two males and four females. One of the males is a Hemingway cat, in that he has six toes on each paw. Two of the females are mostly black, having only small white markings on their chests. Otherwise, the markings are very similar. Off the cuff, I begin assigning names based on the people who have thus far helped with their rescue; Jon, George, Val and Donna. I leave the two mostly black female kittens to be named later. Now it is Momma cat's turn for a name. I don't know why but I tell the staff her name should be Grace. It just popped into my head and it fits her personality as I have seen it so far. Our final instructions are to wean the kittens off of Grace and that as long as they continue to eat kitten food well; they can go to new homes. When I try to settle up the bill again, the vet tells me to bring Grace back in after her milk has dried up. We'll spay her and then discuss payment. When I start to protest, the vet says,

"Let's just call this our part of the community project rescuing these cats has already become."

I can't argue with that. So I smile and tell them I'll see them in a few weeks, when Grace is ready to be spayed.

Right away, I treat all the cats for their fleas and then begin to separate the kittens from Grace. Sometimes bringing the kittens downstairs for play time, other times bringing Grace down. She does not take the separation very well, pacing and meowing, until re-united. The kittens do not show any distress over the separation and only appear to nurse out of convenience or habit. We learn very quickly, that bringing all six kittens downstairs in mass is absolute chaos. Nothing is off limits to them. Everything is a toy. Zippy and Maya take great interest in all the activity and actually look bewildered at their antics. Maya proves to be very nurturing, spending most of her time trying to herd the kittens into a group where she can watch over them. Of course, this is a futile activity with six, six week old kittens. She does not give up her attempts. Zippy tries to teach the kittens to race around the dining room table, like he did with Cricket, not one of them has fully gotten the concept. They pounce on him, attack his tail, climb on him and race back and forth at random. Basically, they have no structure or sense of purpose yet.

The next few days bring us all into a new daily routine that includes a lot of "kitty-vision." I make up fliers with pictures of each kitten, descriptions of their personalities as well as describing the circumstances of how they came into my possession. As I am going out to start putting fliers up, I stop by the fire department where the guys are overseeing a maintenance project. I update them on how the kittens are doing, explain that they each now have a kitten named after them and that the kittens are ready for new homes. I remind them of their promise to help find homes for the kittens, to which they start to laugh pointing to the maintenance person saying,

"You'll take one, won't you?"

I have to give the guy credit, he does not laugh. He comes over, asking what we are trying to get rid of. I show him one of the fliers and shockingly, he is actually interested. Turns out his daughter wants a kitten. I run back home, bring the kitten named George (the one with an extra toe on each paw) down to the firehouse and he agrees to take him home to his daughter. Amazingly, the first kitten has found a new home and I haven't even put up the fliers yet.

The guys think they have done their part and start to laugh over how easy that was. I tell them they got lucky on that one, we won't be done until all the cats have homes.

"Except for the ones you end up keeping." they respond.

"Nope, I told you before. I'm not keeping any of them and I mean it."

The past week with seven cats using the litter box has reaffirmed to me I do not have a tolerance for the odor anymore and am not willing to commit to that chore on a long term basis right now. I have heard that technology for litter box odor control has progressed in the past few years, but honestly I'm skeptical on the promised effectiveness.

Grace shows great distress later that evening when there are only five kittens to settle down. She spends pretty much all night looking for and calling the missing kitten. It proves to be a sleep deprived night for all of us. Both dogs are very aware of her anxiety and whimper in commiseration. Thankfully, by morning she seems to have accepted the situation and settles back in to her daily routine. Keeping the kittens from nursing continues to be a struggle. After some close observation, I notice that Grace actually calls the kittens to her and will even lie down in their midst while they are playing. Is she encouraging them to continue nursing? She did lose her kitten early, maybe her instincts are telling her she should still be nursing. I don't know, but we continue on with the same weaning attempts.

The two previously un-named female kittens have proven to be very laid back and affectionate kittens. They both like to be close to people and are quick to snuggle up for petting and naps. In the evenings while watching television, there are now two people, two dogs and two kittens piled on the couch. It works pretty well. These two kittens have earned the names Cuddles and Bug and they end up being the next ones to get new homes. A young woman has seen the flyer, came to see the kittens, can't decide between Cuddles and Bug so, she takes them both. Three kittens placed, three to go.

Grace again, goes through her evening distress, looking for and calling the missing kittens. By morning, she is fine again. The kittens named Jon and Val are the next to go. An independent pet groomer has agreed to put them in her shop to see if anyone is interested in adopting them, leaving just Grace and the kitten named Donna. This kitten was by far, the wildest and craziest kitten of the bunch. She was the instigator, the agitator, the last one to settle down. Now that she is the only kitten, she does not know what to do with herself; she tries to play with Grace, Zip and Maya but doesn't seem to get any satisfaction there. She becomes calmer and actually begins to seek us out for affection, learning the joy of cuddling and being petted. In just a matter of days, Donna goes to a local pet store to find an adopter. Now that there are no more kittens, Grace's distress that evening is the worst of all and lasts for three days before she stops looking for and calling for the kittens. I have sympathy for her loss and try to distract her with play and cat treats. She was a very attentive mother and seems unsure of herself now. Over time, I find something that attracts her attention... a simple drawstring taken from an old hoodie. She plays with this string with wild abandon and even carries it in her mouth dragging it from room to room. No other cat toys or types of string will do. Just that one.

When the final three kittens were taken to the groomer and pet store, I gave both owners assurances that if the kittens were not adopted within a week, I would bring them back home and continue trying to find them homes myself. This was not necessary, as phone calls to both confirm that indeed all three kittens were adopted. Grace has finished grieving and her milk is starting to dry up. Other than the litter box, she fits into our home so easily; I have to confess I am beginning to entertain thoughts of keeping her. Zippy is teaching her to race around the dining room table and Maya has started sharing her fuzzy tail tennis ball. She still shows no interest in going outside. The closest she comes to outside, is to sit at the front storm door looking out. She will not lay on either of our beds and has taken to lying in the dog bed with the dogs. The most amazing thing to watch is the two dogs moving aside for one cat to eat from their food dishes. Seeing Maya defer to Grace over food is heart-warming. All the work to decrease her previous food aggression has paid off.

During a conversation with another town employee, I confess that I am tempted to keep

Momma Grace when she admits that she has been thinking about it too. We both share that we have reservations about having another house cat for very similar reasons but that, this particular cat has somehow touched our heartstrings. We agree to wait until after she is spayed, put up new fliers for her and if after two weeks nobody has come to adopt her, we'll discuss her future again.

Grace's milk has now dried up enough to take her in to be spayed. The day of the procedure, the vet gives her a thorough exam, pronounces her to be fully recovered and then asks how she is doing in the home. I give her a run down on how she is adapting so well that I, as well as one other person are considering keeping her. Surprisingly, the vet then offers to also take her if no one else decides to adopt her saying,

"There is something about this cat. She has a calm, accepting personality. She touches people."

I agree, "She does get to you. Even my dogs are attached to her. I just don't know how she could have ended up in the situation she was in."

"Let it go. We will never know those answers. Fortunately the right people came across her at the right time and now she is going to have a better future."

The surgery and recovery go very well and it is

time to put the flyers up. As with the kittens, I put a nice picture of Grace on the flyer along with a description of her personality and the circumstances leading to her needing a good, new, loving home. Within a matter of days, I have a call from an interested person. I am determined to make sure Grace goes to the best home possible, so I ask detailed questions about the home environment and why they are interested in Grace in particular. The woman responds that she read the flyer and was touched by her story. They are empty-nesters with an aging house dog and feel they can give Grace the love and care she deserves. I feel confident enough to set up a time for them to come and meet her in person the next day. Upon meeting them, they appear to be very capable, good hearted people. Grace is curious and affectionate with them. They are both impressed with her and Grace goes home with them that very day. I send along the remaining food I had purchased for her as well as a package of cat treats and of course, her string. I explain to the couple her affinity for this particular string over all other playthings.

I am both, sad and happy, relieved, that all of the cats, have gotten new homes, but already feeling, an unexpected emptiness to the house. The dogs also, are feeling the loss of the cats around the house; they both look for Grace, for a few days, before, starting to take notice and an interest in other cats, around the neighborhood. Zippy has always noticed other people's cats, whenever going for a walk, but now Maya is also looking for cats, on our walks. When a cat is spotted, they whine excitedly, and pull eagerly on the leashes, unfortunately for them, the cats don't realize they only want to play.

A week after Grace's departure from our home, I call her new owners to make sure she has adjusted to her new home, is doing well and that they are pleased with their decision to adopt her. The new owner relates that Grace hid for the first two days only coming out at night, but has now slowly accepted them, their dog and the new environment. She continues to play with her string and they are quite pleased with her addition to their home. I feel a great sense of satisfaction for having helped her and the kittens along to better lives, but also just a tiny sense of disappointment that Grace's new owners are indeed a good fit for her. Apparently, I had an unconscious desire to possibly offer to bring her back to my home if things were not going well.

CHAPTER 4

MAYA HAS JUST turned three years old and we celebrate with our usual trip to the pet store and a day out at the park. Both dogs have come to recognize this routine as something special. Of course, they don't know it is a birthday celebration and they don't know whose special day it is, but they do enjoy themselves regardless. Whenever we take the dogs out, they draw a lot of attention from people we encounter. Today is no exception. We get comments on what a perfectly matched pair they are and then there are some people who never knew there was a long-haired variety of dachshund, asking what breed mix Maya is. I always respond with an explanation that she is indeed a pure bred dachshund and that there are actually three hair coats for dachshunds and two separate sizes.

It is again time for Zip to go to the vet for his annual dental cleaning. Still as a preventative measure, due to the tilt of his teeth and heavy tartar build up. This time, it turns out that his age is starting to catch up with him. He has one tooth that is loose and needs to be removed. Luckily, it is one of the very small ones at the bottom front of his mouth and won't cause him any trouble in the future with eating or chewing on bones once it is removed.

While Zip is at the vet, Maya is pretty much lost without her guiding side-kick. She is quiet and subdued, just waiting for the light of her life to return. After picking Wayne up from school, we all head to the vet's office, Wayne and Maya wait in the car while I go in to retrieve Zip, his post care instructions and antibiotics. Once back at the car, Maya wants so badly to greet him with her "kissy wiggle" but senses immediately this is not the time for an enthusiastic show of affection. She settles instead, for a few maternal licks around the muzzle and lying protectively beside him on the seat.

I am having some excavating work done on the yard this summer, in order to have a new retaining wall built behind the house. The dogs find any work around the house to be great entertainment. This job is no exception. There is a lot to investigate at the end of each work day; new smells, altered terrain and many new and interesting items are unearthed. Typical of a house built in the early 1900's, the old outhouse, well and root cellar were filled in with household garbage of the time. Therefore, the yard is now littered with old bottles, dishes, buttons, and marbles mostly broken into small pieces. Due to this debris, I do not allow the dogs outside unattended and we spend every evening picking up these hazards until the excavating work is done. After the digging is done and the footer for the wall is dug, we have a couple of day's reprieve before the footer is to be poured. Wouldn't you know, we get a massive rainstorm. The footer becomes a moat and a significant portion of the excavated dirt wall collapses, sliding into the footer/moat. To me this is an absolute nightmare. To the dogs; it is a wonderful new playground, complete with a wading area, mud puddles and a slip and slide. We borrow a well pump from a neighbor to get the standing water out of the footer. This also is great fun for the dogs. They bark and pounce at us, as we are standing knee deep in water and mud, repeatedly run and tromp through the discharging stream of water. Thankfully we get the water cleared out and the footer is poured. After it has set, the workers return and begin constructing the cinder block retaining wall. Maya is not comfortable with that many strangers in her yard and she sits back at a distance, warily watching the work. Zip on the other hand thinks he is the absolute supervisor, standing atop the dirt wall looking down at the work in progress. As the cinder block wall gets higher, he patrols from one end to the other, inspecting every block as it is laid. After the wall is completed, drains are installed, but we need to wait a bit before gravel and dirt backfill can be brought in.

During this brief period of time, the dogs decide it is great fun to explore the space between the dirt wall and retaining wall. Remembering the moat and mud slide from the rainstorm, I realize this is not a good activity for the dogs. I have to block off the ends of the void for the time being. Extra pieces of fence do the job quite nicely. After what seems an eternity since this project began, the space behind the wall is backfilled, all the debris is cleaned up and the yard is re-seeded. Now we just have to wait for the grass to grow and put an end to the muddy paw prints from the back door through the kitchen to various points in the house. Wiping the dog's paws and mopping the floors twice a day anyway is getting old now.

A few weeks after this project is done, we are over for our usual family Sunday dinner. Another family member has brought her two big dogs along and today there are six small dogs, two big dogs and six people in the house. We are having a pleasant dinner when with no warning, Maya and Casey, the husky mix, get into a fight. We are all shocked. These dogs have all been together many times before and never had any problems getting along. Jamie grabs hold of Casey's collar, pulling her back and away from Maya, who I scoop up into my arms. Casey is placed outside while I begin to check Maya over carefully. I notice one side of her upper lip is puffy and irritated looking. Closer inspection shows a yellowish discharge from the inside of her lip that has a strong odor to it. For the rest of the afternoon, we keep the big dogs separated from the little ones and upon returning home I use my finger to rub a little hydrogen peroxide over the irritated area. Maya accepts this treatment with no issues and I resign myself to yet another trip to the vet's office tomorrow morning.

This is almost becoming a pattern, drop Wayne off at school and head to the vet's office. A thorough exam shows, she has somehow, chipped a molar tooth and it has now become abscessed. The amount of infection shows that this is at least a few days old and did not result from the incident with Casey. It may have actually been the catalyst for the fight if Maya was reacting to Casey bumping into the sore area. Since dental work at our vet's office is normally done Tuesday's anyway, I leave Maya there. She will have the remnants of the chipped tooth removed in the morning.

Zippy is upset when I return home without Maya, spending the remainder of the day watching me expectantly. Every time I move, he races to the front door, only to visibly show disappointment when we do not go through the door. When it is time to go pick Wayne up from school, Zip's excitement is almost uncontainable. I feel sorry for the poor guy, knowing he expects we are going to go to wherever Maya is and bring her back home. Wayne is also worried when he gets in the car and sees that Maya is not there. I explain to him the circumstances with her tooth, adding that she will come home tomorrow feeling so much better. Zip's mood is obvious; he spends the rest of the evening in his dog bed, gloomily watching us. At first he ignores his food but then after a few hours, he tiptoes into the kitchen and eats most of his supper quietly. He is still easily upset and reacts dramatically to changes in his normal routine.

The next day proves to elicit the same behavior from Zip. Around two o'clock the vet's office calls to report that Maya came through her procedure with no complications, is recovering well and I can pick her up between four and five. I have Wayne ride along to hold her on the trip home and we decide it might be best for Zip to stay home. Their reunion will probably be easier on everybody if it is in the comfort of their usual environment. At the vet's office, the doctor comes out to speak with me and shows me the tooth he removed. It was split right down the center all the way through to the root and came out very easily and in two separate pieces. He explained that was a rather significant injury and that an untreated broken tooth can spread infection to the brain and in some cases lead to death. After explaining about the debris in the backyard, the doctor agrees it is possible Maya found something that I had overlooked... but not necessarily the only possibility. He shared that even the best toys and bones can lead to broken or chipped teeth in certain dogs and situations but that eliminating all potential hazards is impossible and not even warranted at this point. This is probably just one of those unexpected things dogs manage to get into.

One of the vet tech's then brings Maya in to the exam room and we are greeted with her patented "kissy wiggle" routine, bringing chuckles of laughter from the vet and his tech, both. After she settles down a little, I am given her antibiotics and instructions for her at home care. An uneventful ride home snuggled in Wayne's lap Maya repeats her "kissy wiggle" with Zip. When he tries to sniff her muzzle, the playful greeting ends abruptly with her soft growl of warning. The rest of the evening is spent quietly, even though Maya shows no lingering after affects from the anesthesia and other than the round of antibiotics, Maya slides' right into her normal routine without batting an eye. It appears Maya had to one up Zip. Just two months ago, he had a little tooth removed; she had to get a bigger one removed.

Over the summer, I realize it has been awhile since we have visited Bonnie & Roger and we make plans one weekend to make the two hour drive and spend the day together. Zip and Maya also make the trip and are thrilled to realize, the farm is our final destination. The expansive rolling hills are comfortably familiar to Zip and hold a bounty of unfinished exploration for Maya, who has only been here once before. In the past, there have been hunting Beagles on the farm and one elderly Shih Tzu house dog now; there is only one Beagle and two young Shih Tzu's inside. This is the first meeting for Zip and Maya and the Shih Tzu's, Oscar and Shelly. All four get along very well and it does not take long for the romping and cavorting to be unleashed. Maya is not as enthusiastic in her play as the other three. Her cautious demeanor is evident today, but she does appear to be comfortable and enjoying her explorations of every nook and cranny of the farm. Zip provides his knowledge and guidance of the best places to explore as well as areas to be avoided. The cow pasture is the top of that list as far as he is concerned. From the first time he encountered the sight of the cows, Zip had no desire to meet them up close and personal. Maya follows his cue and keeps her distance as well.

The start of supper preparations ends the dog's explorations. All four keep close to the enticing smells coming from the grill. Zip recognizes this as beef he is far more capable of tackling compared to the type still on the hoof in the pasture. We all enjoy our meal and after cleaning up, sit down to watch a TV program. All four dogs are used to stretching out on the couch during this time. Unfortunately however, everybody cannot fit onto one couch. There is some shuffling for prime position. Zip tries to assume his old spot beside Roger where he can lick his elbow. Oscar is not sure if he wants to allow this and tries uncertainly to reclaim his owner. Zip pays him no concern what so ever and Oscar decides to lay down about a foot away keeping an eye on the situation. Maya and Shelly have no problem deciding where to settle down. Maya is in my lap, while Shelly is on Bonnie's. Oscar eventually gives up on his observation of Zip and assumes his normal position on the back of the couch where he can watch out the window for any invaders leaving Roger's elbow open for all of Zip's attention.

It is now early September, Maya has just turned four years old and while washing dishes one evening, I hear part of a story on the local news about the SPCA busting a puppy mill operation right here in West Virginia, seizing over 1,000 dogs. By the time I get into the living room, the piece is over and I go back to my dishes shaking my head over the huge number of dogs reported to be affected. I know these facilities exist and feel naïve over my initial surprise that one was reportedly operating in our state. Maybe tomorrow mornings news will repeat the story and I can learn more about the situation.

The next day, I have forgotten about the story and am caught off guard when indeed the morning news repeats the same story that I missed the previous evening, in its entirety. There are no specific details in this piece as to where this facility was located, but just the knowledge of what those dogs lives were probably like is saddening. I realize that given the numerous remote mountains and valleys throughout the state, it shouldn't be so surprising that something so large could go undetected. I'll make a point to watch the evening news tonight and see if there are any more details. Maybe, there will be something we can do to help.

The evening news does provide new information and as I am sitting on the couch with Maya lying beside me, I start to feel myself stiffen up when I hear the location of this "puppy mill." Then become numb when I hear that the majority of dogs seized were dachshunds. Then when the news anchor reports the name of the owner/operator, I am at first dumbfounded, but quickly slide into denial mode. Muttering out loud to myself,

"No, no, it can't be. I know that name is familiar, but please oh please don't let it be what I think it is. Please no, I've got to be wrong. I'm mixing names up again, right."

CHAPTER 5

A QUICK RETRIEVAL of the dog's papers confirms I am not mixing names up. My heart drops into my stomach. There on Maya's papers, is the black and white confirmation my initial suspicion is true. The name of the owner of the puppy mill in the news piece is the same name listed on Maya's registration and bill of sale papers. Also still in her health record folder, one of two business cards given to me when I purchased Maya. The other card had been given to the secretary at Wayne's school when she had inquired about who we had gotten Maya from. I vaguely recall running in to her some months later outside a convenience store and that we had a brief conversation where she informed me that she did indeed purchase a male littermate of Maya's. My head is swimming with questions now that I have confirmation. Maya did come from the very type of situation I had tried so hard to avoid and not only did I inadvertently support this operation myself, I actually sent someone else there as well.

How? How could this be? Even though I recall the initial phone conversation with the "breeder" as being very detailed, professional and caring; surely upon arriving at the location I would have seen some evidence of the magnitude of her operation wouldn't I? I was there on the property and searching my memory, I cannot piece together the details in the news report with what I saw. The house I went to was not out in the country, it was in a nice suburban housing area just outside of a major city. A facility housing the thousand dogs reported in the news piece should have been visible to any visitors and certainly any neighbors should have been aware of that many dogs. Even with the proof right in front of me, a small voice in the back of my head still tries to assert I may be wrong. I know logically I heard correctly. It is the same city and the same breeder name. But emotionally I am looking for evidence that there is some sort of mix up. They could not have gone from the small number of dogs I viewed on my visit to over a thousand in just a few years. It just doesn't fit. Either it is a different "breeder" or I missed something big while on the property.

At my computer I check the news channels website to further confirm the information is correct. It is. Further searching leads me to the nearby city's newspaper and television coverage providing additional details and pictures. It does not take long before I have some serious regret over viewing the pictures and reading the more complete report of the conditions this "breeder" subjected these dogs to. In horrified shock, I view picture after picture showing dog's in various states of neglect, cruel confinement and terrible sanitation. Most of the pictures show the inside of the facility. I still have no idea where on the property this building was. I do not recognize it at all from my brief visit there. A few of the pictures show the immediate surrounding area and I can clearly see both the house and the garage that I do remember, visible in the background. This is the same place. There is no doubt in my mind now. The house and garage pictured are exactly as I remembered them.

After about an hour of viewing all the available coverage, I begin to look at the pictures again. This time looking closely at the individual dog's in the photos, two pictures in particular are especially haunting to me. One of the photos shows a very small black & tan, long haired dachshund puppy in an elevated wire mesh cage, trying to stand with all four paws on a very small square of plywood in the center of the cage floor. Even though this is a young puppy, all four paws do not fit onto the plywood square. I can't help but wonder; did Maya and her littermates also try to relieve the discomfort of standing on nothing but wire mesh in this same manner. How sad for a dog to never feel the cool cushion of grass between their toes, never feel the tickle of individual blades brushing against the belly and never smell the sweet aroma of freshly cut grass.

The other picture shows an adult dog, reported to be six or seven years old, experiencing the feel of the grass for the first time. It is reported that several of the older dogs were either fearful or flat out refused to walk on the grass. It was such an unknown surface to them they didn't know how to react. Were Maya's parents included in those dogs? Were any of her littermates still there? So many questions. Had I not bought Maya would she still be there? Neglected, ignored and denied all of the things that bring her such joy now? Would anybody have ever seen that impish glint in her eye, felt how perfectly her head fits under the chin when she snuggles on the couch beside you? How many other Maya's were still there having no idea of what the world is really like?

I look down at Maya curled up asleep under my chair and have a bit of a break-down. I scoop her up from her slumber, hug her tight and begin to sob, telling her how sorry I am for the first weeks of her life. I would never want any living creature to live such an existence and feel horrible that this little ray of sunshine in our lives was subject to such misery, all because of another human being.

I shut down the computer, but can't seem to let go of Maya. I cuddle her close for the rest of the evening, sniffling off and on. She seems a bit confused but allows me to try infusing her with as much extra love as possible. No adored and pampered pet is going to resist that kind of attention, even if they don't know the source. At some point during the evening, I realize that most likely both of my dogs were born into this same environment. Zippy now gets coaxed into my almost desperate display of affection. He is not so inclined to tolerate my indulgence. He is far too aware of my moods and finds any type of mood swing to be highly upsetting. I feel him begin to tremble against my arms and realize, neither dog is able to understand the upsetting information I learned today and that I am probably causing at least Zippy some distress by exposing them to my emotional outburst. I force myself to relax, release my grip on both dogs and let them go to their normal evening spots. I am bothered for the rest of the night, having trouble falling asleep and experiencing several bad dreams before waking up to the realization that, I am angry.

A fresh day provides enough perspective to understand that I am actually angry at being deceived by the "breeder" and ashamed to be witness to another human being's self-satisfying use of animals that have done nothing to deserve such callous treatment and confinement. These dogs lived an existence devoid of any type of enjoyment and affection, lacking in the simplest basic care they are totally dependent on the human to provide, for what, financial gain? I have to question even that motive because if there were over 1,000 dogs, how many were being sold? Having bred yellow lab puppies briefly, when Wayne was a baby, I understand the expense and care required to breed just one female dog and raise one litter of puppies at a time. I don't see how such a large scale operation can yield happy, healthy puppies, nor be profitable financially.

Monday at work, I suddenly realize, some of the employees in another branch of our organization live in the same city where the "puppy mill" was located. Knowing one of them to be a dog lover and having met Zip and Maya, I give him a call. He is horrified to learn that this facility is where Maya came from and he divulges everything he has learned thus far. It turns out, he actually knows the "breeder's" adult daughter and has already spoken to her about the accusations in the news. He relates that, according to the daughter and other local residents this "breeder" has been in the business for over 30 years (she did claim this when I spoke to her and has it listed on her business card) and started out being a very careful, compassionate and respected breeder of several small breeds of dogs, but primarily dachshunds. Over the past few years, she put less and less effort into finding homes for the puppies yet continuing to breed litter after litter. The daughter also reports that the family tried to intervene numerous times, taking it upon themselves to help find homes for the puppies whenever possible and encouraging the "breeder" to follow-up on calls and e-mails of people looking for puppies. They knew it was a deteriorating situation but where met with resistance and denial from the "breeder" over how bad it actually was. In some small way, this information gives me a little sense of relief, in that she at least had started out in a responsible, compassionate manner. Perhaps she had other issues that led to her irresponsible behaviors, never the less it does not negate the reality of today's situation, in anyway.

Continued conversation also solves the question of how I could have actually been on the premises and not noticed any clue to the actual conditions described in the news. I recall vividly the layout of the property visible during my visit. Pulling up a slight hill in to the driveway led to a garage directly in front with the house sitting off to the left, accessible by a walkway from the driveway. Parking on the driveway in front of the garage, which was on the crest of the hill, we walked over to the house on the walkway only seeing what was on this side of the hill. Apparently, from my contact's explanation the kennel's that housed the dogs, were on the back side of the hill behind the garage. They were not visible from the main portion of the property and I suspect were the actual source of the numerous barking dogs I heard prior to leaving the property and had dismissed when distracted and hurried along by the "breeder" who had to get to that out of state wedding. Right, sure. You bet I have to wonder about that now, was that just a ploy to get us off the property as quickly as possible.

Even though this "breeder" may have started out in a respected manner and there may have been unknown circumstances leading her down the wrong path, I feel there was a certain level of awareness that what she was doing was not acceptable. Otherwise why would it be necessary to be evasive, vague and deceptive with potential new owners, if she knew she had an acceptable practice going on? Full disclosure would have been welcome. Reportedly the SPCA was eventually brought in by the city after they had received numerous complaints by the neighbor's regarding over-powering odors coming from the property. It also apparently took a significant amount of time and investigation before anyone in a position of authority recognized the severity of what was truly going on at that property.

I thank my acquaintance for his information and he promises to let me know if he hears of anything else I, as an owner of one of her dogs, should know or can do to help the dogs involved in the seizure. Over the next few weeks, there are continued news updates on the progress of the dogs rescued and my emotion's begin to settle down, allowing me to realize that even though Maya may have had a less than desirable start, her life now is the polar opposite and she has already been given everything any dog could desire. She, along with the littermate, I referred the school secretary to, are two of the lucky ones. Maya is living a life that encompasses the best of human companionship. I truly believe her littermate is too, though I have not encountered his owners again since the chance meeting at the convenience store.

It is during this time of realization that the news is now reporting the rescued dogs will be offered up for adoption. The SPCA has relocated all of the adult dogs and special needs puppies to other shelter's around the country for any medical and rehabilitation needs they may have. All of the healthy puppies will remain in the shelter that handled the initial seizure and adopted out to approved local adopters. I am pleased that all of the SPCA's national resources are being brought to help these dogs and that the very best efforts are being used to bring each dog into the most fulfilling life possible.

Further reflection leads me to the conclusion that we saved one, no two, of her puppies, albeit unknowingly. We now can make a conscious choice to save another. Looking about at our home, the yard and thinking over our financial resources, I feel we have plenty of room, love and resources available to add one more dog to our family.

I do not act on this thought right away. I force myself to think it over for 24 hours then after weighing the pros and cons, decide whether to act or not. I do weigh all the possibilities carefully and of course, do not change my mind. We do have the resources and love to show one more doxie just how good life with people can be. I get online and begin the formal application process; which is to complete an application providing all of our contact information, vet's contact information, references and a brief description of what we can offer to one of these puppies. I add an additional paragraph explaining that I am already the owner of two dachshunds, one of which I had acquired from the same "breeder" with the circumstances of that purchase, clearly defined and that I am experienced with this breed and the needs one of these puppies will have.

A few days later, we receive an e-mail response that due to an overwhelming number of interested applicants, potential adopters are asked to come to the shelter on specified days. There we would view the available puppies. Choosing no more than three puppies of interest and fill out a form stating which puppies we would wish to adopt. Then, all of the applications for each individual puppy would be reviewed and the best local adopter for each individual puppy would be selected. The posted information keeps saying local adopters, I am unclear if we are considered to be local or not. We are after all, a two hour drive away yet still within the state. I e-mail the shelter with my question and after two days with no response, I try calling the shelter directly numerous times. Only to get a pre-recorded message stating that, due to the over-whelming amount of calls for the puppies any potential adopters should submit an on-line application for adoption and follow the ensuing directives. I have already done all of that and am just being sent in circles now. So, I guess since the visitation day is only a week away, we will make the drive, choose which puppies catch our attention and hope for the best.

I am starting to envision what our home will be like with another puppy to enjoy, when the evening news reports that the puppies at the shelter are in desperate need of toys, bones and treats. Apparently, they have exhausted the shelter's supplies and are bored with sitting in their cages with nothing to entertain them. A glance at the basket holding Zippy and Maya's toys, gives me an easy idea to help alleviate that problem. Sorting through the basket, in no time, I gather a grocery store bag full of items that my two do not play with. If I gathered up that many, I bet if I call a couple of other dog owners and dog lovers, collectively we could come up with a good supply of toys. A few calls that evening and a few conversations the next day, soon we have gathered up enough toys to fill a good sized box. We then add a few pouches of new treats and rawhides to complete the package and mail it to the shelter with a little note of good wishes for all the puppies.

The day of the puppy selection has arrived. It is a beautiful September morning for a long car ride. As per the e-mailed instructions we received, we have left Zip and Maya at home. The puppies, it is explained, will be stressed and over-whelmed as it is by the visiting people. Additional dogs will only compound their anxiety it is believed by the shelter staff. I understand that completely and also think there is the potential for exposing all of the dogs to unnecessary health risks. Upon locating the shelter, we are directed to park in a lot almost a quarter mile down the road. Both sides of the road and all the surrounding parking areas are lined with cars and we pass multiple groups of people walking toward the shelter where we can see a line of already waiting people even though the actual time for admission is still a half an hour away. I am soon grateful for the moderate fall temperature this Saturday as we take our place in what seems an impossibly long line. We very well may be here all day, from the early looks of it.

Everyone is chatting excitedly. There are many personal stories told and also some gossip from supposedly knowledgeable sources about the puppies and the seizure in general. Some of which seem so outlandish, they cannot possibly be true. But yet others are collaborated on by multiple people in line and therefore may be true. The most agreed upon of these gossip stories is that, even though there is a fenced in area for the dogs at the shelter to romp around in, the puppies are no longer permitted in this area. Supposedly, there were large groups of people gathering around the yard and two puppies were actually stolen right out of the yard in broad daylight shortly after they had first arrived. Because of that incident and an attempted break-in of the facility, the puppies had 24 hour security guards patrolling the shelter grounds. What a mess. If any of that was actually true, who knows. I do know that puppies have been stolen from pet stores, so I suppose that is possible as well.

Finally after two hours in line, it is our turn to go in. The shelter workers are admitting only five people at a time so that there are never more than 15 people in with the puppies at any time. When one group leaves, the next group is allowed in. As we approach the facility housing the pups, we are given a selection form with three lines on it for our three top puppy selections and our contact information. The gate, through which we are admitted, is about thirty feet away from the entrance to the facility. After this short walk and before entering the building, we are met by another shelter worker, who checks that we do have our selection form before being admitted to the building. Entering the building housing the puppies turns out to be a bit of a visual over load. I knew the large number of dogs reported to have been removed from the "breeders" possession, but upon seeing row after row of cages containing just the puppies, the true magnitude of the seizure becomes sadly apparent. Wayne and I look at each other, both over-whelmed, when he whispers to me,

"Mom, there are so many. How are we ever going to pick just three?"

"I don't know. I really wasn't expecting this. Let's just take a deep breath and try our best."

We both take a calming breath and then take our first step into this unbelievable world of needy puppies. I am immediately impressed with the quality of care these puppies are now under. Each puppy is clean and well groomed, each cage is also spotlessly clean and there are shelter representatives stationed about every 10 feet or so to monitor the puppies and provide assistance if needed. The amount of resources needed to get these puppies to this point is almost staggering when I stop to think about it. I re-focus myself to see each puppy for the individual they are and not as a part of the whole sad situation they came from.

The first cage we come to holds a litter of 3 twelve week old pups. One little long-haired female in particular, catches my attention right away. She has a unique coloring that I have not seen in a dachshund before. The main body coloring is the color of caramel and her accent markings are light beige. She reminds me of the old caramel candy with vanilla icing in the center that I loved as a kid. Not only does her coloring catch my attention, so does her personality. She has that same impish glint in her eyes that Maya had at that age and still has today. She shows interest in us, coming up to sniff our hands, then pouncing back to grab a little stuffed toy in her cage. I can't help smiling at her antics. Surely, the very first cage we look at is not going to contain the one pup for us. We have to keep moving through the aisles and give every pup a chance.

Up one aisle, looking on both sides then down another aisle... cage after cage, most holding more than one puppy, nobody catches our attention again until the beginning of the very last row. There side by side, in separate cages are two red, long-haired females that are listed as sisters and being nine months old. They are both timid, but do show interest when we talk to them and are truly beautiful looking dogs. They are added to my mental list of possibilities. The remaining cages do not contain anybody who catches our attention again.

Before writing down our final selections on our form, we walk back through one more time, making sure of our initial choices and that we have not missed anybody. That first little pup remains just as endearing as the first time we looked at her. We quickly agree she is our first choice, then move back over to the sisters. While we are standing in front of their cages debating which one should be listed as our second choice, Wayne holds his hand up to the front of both cages, and the one on the left actually starts to stretch her nose forward to sniff in his direction. She becomes our second selection. Her sister, who is now making tentative eye contact with me, is our third choice.

At the exit to the facility, we turn in our selection form and a printed copy of our initial application to a shelter volunteer, who reviews the documents. She notices that we already have two dachshunds and after a few minutes discussion about our dogs and the circumstances of Maya coming from this same "breeder" she marks our application with a large smiley face, explaining this is their signal to the reviewing staff designating this potential adopter as favorable. All right, that's another positive step. Wayne and I exit the building and watch as the next group enters. We have done all we can now. The final decision is out of our hands. On the ride home, we discuss the three pups we picked out and start to think up possible names for each of them.

The following day is our normal Sunday dinner

and while there, we share our experience of the previous day. The enormity of the number of puppies to be placed and the three pups we decided on. While describing the first little pup, so full of herself and sassy like Maya, it occurs to me why her coloring is so appealing to me. As a child, I had a stuffed monkey I called "Chimpy" whose markings were the exact same colors as that little pups. I begin referring to her as the "Chimpy Pup."

Over the next two weeks, we go about our normal routines, yet always wondering in the back of our minds if there will be a phone call informing us we have been chosen to adopt one of the puppies. Every e-mail and phone message is reviewed with bated breath and at one point during this time, I run into our Vet's office to pick up a new bottle of Frontline. I mention to the receptionist that we have applied to adopt one of the puppies from the seizure and inform her they may call to verify our status as active patients there. The receptionist instantly nod's her head and reports they have already received a phone call to verify our account, as well as another potential adoptive family here in this area. She smiles, wishes me good luck and I take that as yet another positive step in our favor.

Unfortunately, after several more weeks have passed, there has been no phone call or e-mail and a check of the shelter's website displays a banner announcing that all of the puppies have been successfully adopted into new homes. I am a bit saddened... there will not be a new puppy in our house after all. I break the news to Wayne, who is also a little sad, but reports,

"It's okay, it's not like we don't have a dog at all."

This saddening realization does not lessen the love and enjoyment received by Zip and Maya in anyway, if anything it strengthens our devotion to them. We are perfectly content with the knowledge that we offered our home to a puppy in need and that there were more than enough loving homes to place all of them in. Where I am certain, they will enjoy lives leaps and bounds more fulfilling than what they were born in to. Zip and Maya are both testaments that even though a dog may have come from less than ideal beginnings they are resilient enough to embrace change and prosper in the care of a loving family.

CHAPTER 6

WAYNE is about to begin his Senior Year of high school and Maya is about to turn five years old. Time sure does escape for all of us. Like all parents at this time in their child's life, I can't help reflecting on the impending end of my only child's days of being a child and his coming into manhood. Of course, he still has his moments of juvenile behavior, but those are becoming fewer and fewer. I find myself staring at him, wondering who this deep-voiced young man before me is. Where is the innocent babe I held in my arms so many times? Yet, as I continue to watch, I see the child he was deep in his eyes as well as the man he is becoming and I am equally proud of them both.

Maya continues to see him as "her boy," greeting him with the same "kissy wiggle" as five years ago. Zip appears to have elevated him to co-master status now. He responds to Wayne's direction and commands on an equal level as he does mine. During this summer of transition, Zip goes in to the vet for his teeth cleaning, ending up having two more small teeth removed; now giving him a gap-tooth grin when he opens his mouth. While Zip is having his dental work done, Wayne is scheduled to have his Senior Pictures taken and about half way through the session the photographer asks about Wayne's interests or any places he enjoys visiting that are nearby that could be incorporated into his pictures. A few minutes of discussion lead Wayne to ask if his dog can be in the pictures. Absolutely, is the response from the photographer. I run back to the house, gather up Maya and her brush and am back before they have finished the setting they were shooting when I left.

Maya is so eager to be with Wayne, I can hardly hold her still long enough to run the brush through her. The photographer has Wayne sit under a tree out on the lawn holding Maya in his arms. She is too excited and none of these shots end up being very good, but letting her roam around a few minutes settles her down. By this time, Wayne has leaned over, propped on his bent arm head resting on his hand. Maya goes over to him, snuggles herself tight against him and gazes up at him adoringly. The photographer starts snapping pictures and many of these shots turn out very nicely. It now seems perfectly fitting that Maya be in this photo shoot. Wayne is after all, "her boy" and she has shared so many other milestone events with him since she joined our family.

The final school year progresses easily with all

the typical Senior Year activities and events. Until the flu season begins. During the peak of a particularly bad flu outbreak, Wayne comes down with the flu for the first time in his life. It hits him hard and fast. He spikes a fever of 105 degrees that I cannot bring down at home. A trip to the ER, IV fluids and fever reducers get the fever down and he is sent home to finish recuperating. He remains sick for a while, missing a full week of school for the first time in all of his school years. During this illness, Maya shows great concern. She knows, "her boy" is not feeling well. She calmly lies at his side staring at him every so often, following his every move and being very sedate. Her concern is obvious and she does not let her guard down for an entire week. Gradually he begins to regain his strength and return to normal. Maya continues to watch him carefully, but as he improves more and more, she begins to relax and resume her typical carefree, playful attitude. She seems to know her antics amuse him, yet she also seems to know to temper her games to levels he is able to meet. It is intriguing to see such maternal instinct from her even though she was spayed before she ever came into heat and certainly, other than the kittens, had no opportunity to practice mothering skills.

The school year is at an end, graduation is upon us. Since Wayne is the oldest grandchild, many members of our family will be traveling from Pennsylvania to attend his graduation ceremony. Past experiences have shown that Maya gets overwhelmed by large groups of people and this will be a trying few days for her, but she has been showing improvement in her tolerance, we'll manage just fine. The first wave to arrive is my sister and her five kids, who have been here several times before and are familiar to both dogs. Zippy is excited to see the kids. Maya is cautious and wary of all the commotion, trying to position herself safely behind my legs. As the number of people in the house increases, Maya actually becomes calmer. All of the additional guests are adults. She appears to recognize there are enough adults to watch the children now and she doesn't have to and can relax. After the graduation ceremony, we all return to the house and after a few hours visiting, begin to decide sleeping arrangements. Wayne's father leaves to stay in a motel. Wayne and the two boys are in his room. Nana and Aunt Jane are in the guest room. My sister and her three girls are in my room, leaving the dogs and I to take the couch. Since I often fall asleep on the couch anyway, while watching TV, this arrangement is not so new to the dogs. The night passes uneventfully and the following morning's stirrings take Maya by surprise, leading to a round of barking as each person ventures down the stairs.

I have a surprise party planned for later in the day, but need to keep Wayne distracted and the other kids occupied in the meantime. We opt to go to our local park, where the kids and dogs both, can burn of some energy, yet allow the adults to relax while watching the kids. The dogs get walked all over the park multiple times and are an endless source of amusement for the kids when they slide down the sliding board. Finally, the dogs are both utterly exhausted and I bring them under the pavilion with us to rest while the kids continue to play. The adults chat, watching the kids play. The dogs have taken up positions on the picnic table where they can lie down and also watch the kids. Before we know it, it is lunchtime. Heading back to the house, we pick up lunch on the way. The kids then play video games until it is time for the surprise party, which was a surprise and a great time for Wayne. Unfortunately, everybody from Pa. has to leave right after the party for various reasons. When we return to the house, we are alone and can settle back into our normal daily activities.

For the first time in over 14 years, counting kindergarten and preschool, I will no longer have to get up before daylight to assure Wayne is fed, dressed and ready for school. Hurray! I am not naturally a real early morning person, especially in the winter time. I just really hate the sound of the alarm clock on a cold, snowy or rainy day. I am looking forward to this summer, before the onset of the next stage in Wayne's life. We have already planned to spend as much time as possible enjoying the outdoor activities so readily available in our area.

Summer weather has been an issue with Maya pretty much from her first summer with us. She sheds a significant amount of her fur, as well as scratching a lot. I make absolutely sure to apply the flea prevention spray promptly as prescribed every month without fail. Shortly after first bringing her home, she had a small patch of fur on her chest that started coming out even though it was winter then. I had the vet check it out when she went in for her spay and dewclaw removal surgery. He did a skin scraping and found nothing out of order. It may be a slight allergy to something in the house he reported at the time, as long as it did not get any worse, nothing to worry about. That area never did get any worse; the fur never did come back in completely, though. Now with each progressive summer, she has experienced an increase in her scratching and hair loss in other parts of her body, mostly her belly and the insides of her back legs.

This July Maya's skin irritation reaches a new level of severity. She is now developing hot spots along with her scratching and chewing behavior. We are all miserable over her obvious discomfort. Nothing brings her any length of relief. I take her in to the vet, where Dr. Kendrick spends a full hour trying to pinpoint the source of her irritation. Dr. Kendrick came highly recommended and has always shown dedication and true concern for all of my pets. Today, my opinion and regard for his compassion reaches a level that will be difficult for another vet to meet, none the less surpass. I do not exaggerate, when I say he spent a full hour with Maya and I trying to understand what was going on with her skin. He repeatedly examined her carefully, asked me questions about any triggers and her symptoms and then checked reference books in his library. Back and forth he went, over and over, together we come to the conclusion that she has multiple allergies. Most obvious would be a flea bite allergy, but also appears to present with food, indoor and also outdoor allergies.

Dr. Kendrick relates it will be a trial and error process to figure out what treatments will give her the most relief. He gives her a shot today, sends her home with prescription anti-itch shampoo, a topical spray for the hot spots and additional options to add to this regime if needed. The most likely food related possible allergen at this point, appears to be beef proteins. So I will begin immediately to remove beef from her diet, see if that has any result and then if necessary, try the other most common allergens.

The remainder of the summer becomes an almost all consuming effort to alleviate Maya's symptoms. Removing beef from her diet proves to be far more difficult than I first imagined. Even if a dog food is chicken flavored, it does not mean there is no beef in it. Reading the ingredient labels for the various commercial dog foods, I am appalled at the amount of "junk" and chemicals in dog food. Having over the past few years, changed my own eating habits, due to chronic stomach ailments, I realize the food I am giving my dogs is far more unhealthy than what I am eating and decide to start preparing their food myself. It turns out in practice not to be that difficult for our situation, due to the numerous limitations in my diet, they now eat what I eat. I just cook a little bit more and since they are two rather small dogs, it doesn't take that much more food.

By the end of the summer and after much experimentation, it appears we have hit on a fairly good combination. No beef in her diet (not even rawhides or beef flavored treats), aloe and tea tree oil shampoo, followed by a rinse with Aveeno bath treatment every two weeks, topical spray at the first hint of a hot spot, Gold Bond powder when her belly starts turning pink and finally Benadryl to curtail any more difficult episodes all in conjunction with the monthly flea spray. Sometimes, it seems the only thing I get done is manage Maya's allergies, but it pays off, no more visits to Dr. Kendrick are necessary. We make it through the summer without any serious flair-ups.

A new source of anxiety for Maya is making itself evident this summer in conjunction with her increased skin irritations. She is now showing mild stress during thunder storms. I had never observed her fear of loud noises carry over to weather events before now, but it is unmistakable, she rolls her eyes, yawns, licks her lips and is never more than a foot away from me during a storm. I thought she had reached a tolerable level of acceptance for fireworks and try not to encourage an escalation in her new source of anxiety by practicing the same techniques we used before. She does not appear to be overly distraught during storms, just uncomfortable and uncertain.

The onset of fall sees Maya's "boy" begin attending our local state university. Three days a week he catches a ride for his morning classes, the other two days he has evening classes. The dogs and I drop him off and then go to the park or shopping until he is done. There is an athletic park nearby and that becomes our usual stop. Both dogs soon learn every inch of the park and on occasion, we are there during a little league game. Zippy and I are content to watch the little guys play ball. Maya is not. She watches the kids with just a passing glance; the ball however, is another story. She feels compelled to chase that ball. Sitting several yards off the field in bleachers is not far enough. She can see the ball, focuses on it, follows its every move, whining and prancing impatiently. Her desire is amusing and not lost on the other spectators sitting on the bleachers.

Sadly, soon the weather starts turning too cold for evenings at the park. Little league season is over as well, so now while classes are in session, we return home for a little quiet time. The "kissy wiggle" greeting remains the norm each and every time we pick Wayne up and Maya soon begins to catch the attention of departing students, some come over to the car others smile at her antics. This pattern continues on until the college shuts down for winter break.

Christmas this year is at home. As we begin decorating and preparing for the holiday, Zip and Maya both are very familiar with these activities now and take enjoyment in the festivities. Shortly after presents start appearing under the tree, I notice Maya has already begun her rearranging behavior. We learned in previous years this could become an all-consuming activity for us if we insist on putting the presents in any other arrangement, so right away we leave them where she puts them.

After our final shopping excursion and upon returning home, we are greeted by a mass of shredded wrapping paper, scattered all over the living room floor. We both freeze in our tracks, looking at each other, dumbfounded. What in the world happened here? The dogs are still in the midst of their normal greeting routine, hopping up and down, whining excitedly at our return. Today, this routine has an added level of chaos with bits of shredded paper being tossed and scattered about even more.

"What happened here? What did you two get into?" I question the dogs crossly.

Of course I don't expect an answer, but I end up getting one anyway, when Maya darts over to the couch where she retrieves the new toy that was to be Zippy's Christmas present. He then follows suit and comes out from the dining room with the other new toy. This one had been intended for Maya. A quick glance under the tree reveals all the other presents appear to be undisturbed. Setting our purchases down, I coax the dogs outside to do their business and to assess the damage they had actually done. Further inspection shows all five of the presents for the dogs have been opened. Two stuffed toys, two bones and one package of lamb jerky teats. Luckily, they were unable to gain access to the actual treats and bones; otherwise we may have a couple of upset stomachs to deal with as well as the mess of shredded paper.

Even though both dogs are so clearly proud of themselves, like with a child, I don't think they should be rewarded for taking it upon themselves to open their presents on a whim. While they are outside, I pick up their "booty," put it away out of sight and clean up the shredded paper. The plan is to re-wrap the presents and let them open them again on

Christmas morning. When they come back in, they look around a bit, seemingly confused as to what happened to all the hard work they had done and where were the great surprises they had uncovered. They then give up the search and go back to playing with the same old basket full of de-fuzzed, squeaker-less toys that have accumulated over the past few years. Honestly, they have enough toys for a couple dozen dogs to play with. How did they get so spoiled?

On Christmas morning, they re-open their gifts and are pleased all over again to have something new to keep focused on for a while. Maya's stuffed toy this year is a pink and white plush soccer ball that is almost as big as she is. This turns out to be her favorite toy for quite a long time. She will chase after it endlessly and also finds it irresistible when we kick it across the floor for her. Zippy does not bother her ball. She must have set down rules that this one is off limits to him. When she decides to shake it, it takes all over her might to accomplish the feat, as I said it is nearly as big as she is.

New Year's Eve this year shows Maya has made significant progress tolerating the fireworks set off by the neighbors. She barely pays any attention to them at all. Thankfully, patience and maturity have brought Maya past all of the early behavior issues she had. Not that all of her little quirks are gone. She merely tolerates fireworks, I don't think she will ever be comfortable around them and she still thinks she must attack the broom, mop and vacuum, but now a simple "NO" command stops her from advancing.

Now that the holidays are over, we try to get back to our normal routines but Wayne's eyes, which have been of concern for a while and which the doctor has been watching carefully... have deteriorated now to a point where after another check-up it is decided that the time to address the problem is now. Meeting with the eye surgeon at WVU Hospital, it is determined he will need two separate surgeries on his eyes to correct the weakened eyelids and alleviate the chronic dry eye before there is permanent damage to the corneas. He has been through several other surgeries in the past and takes these in stride as well.

The first surgery is for the second week of February. Winter weather has set in with a vengeance. We have had snow after snow after snow for days on end now. Another storm is forecast to come through the day of the first surgery, so Pop Pop goes along to the hospital to do the driving back home and help with Wayne in case he is still groggy from the anesthesia and too much for me to handle by myself. The day surgery procedure goes well and by the time we are headed home, the snow has just started to fall. Looks like we got done, just in time.

Back at the house, it does take both of us to get Wayne safely into the house. Both of his eyes are swollen and bandaged, not to mention he is still unsteady on his feet. From the moment I open the door, Zip and Maya know something is very different. They do not greet us with their normal enthusiasm. Nor, do they bark for Pop Pop to play with them. Zippy has been through one of Wayne's surgeries before. This however, is Maya's first experience with the post-op recovery process. Her maternal instincts come out in full force and immediately. She carefully follows Wayne's assisted progress to the couch. She gently sniffs in the direction of his eyes, never actually touching him; the concern is almost visible on her face. It takes some coaxing to get her to go outside to do her business and when she comes back inside, she positions herself at his feet while he is laying on the couch, resting her chin on his leg. She watches him unmoving, except for an occasional twitch of her nose. This remains her spot for the rest of the day, only leaving when called to eat her supper or go outside.

I had taken two days off from work for the surgery, but the snow storm that hit our area, turned that into four days off. In addition to putting ointment in Wayne's eyes several times during the day, I am kept busy shoveling snow. We are measuring the accumulation in feet now rather than inches. The snow pack is far too much for the dogs to maneuver through, they also need to have a path kept clear for them in the backyard.

Maya continues to monitor Wayne very closely, he is recovering well. She assesses him every morning and night with the same careful sniffing only in the vicinity of his eyes. A week later, we follow-up with the surgeon who confirms, he is indeed healing well and the second surgery is scheduled for the first week of March. In the remaining two weeks of February, the snow is relentless, snowing every day with a monstrous storm at the end of the month that pretty much shuts down the entire area for several days by bringing down numerous trees and power lines, blocking almost every roadway. The National Guard is called in to help with the clean-up and the remnants of the damage remain evident for months to come.

By the end of this storm, the dog's path in the backyard is more like a tunnel, towering far above their heads, with no other avenue available for them to walk through. Maya does not even attempt to scramble up the bank of snow and when she comes in with snowballs stuck to her fur; she simply lies down until they melt on their own. One of the dogs has given up completely on navigating over the ice packed path and has begun to do their business on the back porch. I suspect it is Zip. Given the circumstances I let it go, simply wait until it freezes and then flip the frozen pile off the porch with a garden shovel. He is getting on in years, it doesn't seem fair to expect him to navigate such terrain now and I know it is getting more and more difficult for him.

The second surgery comes just a few days after what turns out to be the last snow storm for this winter. Everything goes well again and Maya repeats the same behavior pattern she displayed with the first surgery. She lies by his side sniffing gently in the direction of his eyes, only leaving him to eat and go outside. After three or four days, she seems satisfied that all is well with him and she relaxes in her vigil, returning to her normal happy go lucky self.

The day before we are to return to the surgeon, we are over for Sunday dinner when I notice, the side of Maya's muzzle looks swollen. Closer inspection reveals the gums and inner lip are swollen and there is the distinctive bad odor I now know to be from infection. Oh dear, here we go again. It seems like she must have broken another tooth. Just how much can happen, when one gets into a funk pattern, is certainly being shown to me. I know we all get into these patterns from time to time and this is not a new experience for me but, that knowledge doesn't always help any of us deal with one crisis after another.

On the way to Wayne's appointment, I take Maya in to the vet; giving my consent to have her examined and go ahead and provide whatever treatment is needed while we are at the hospital. We will return after the other appointment is over. This day just gets harder and harder as it progresses. There is apparently an emergency at the hospital requiring the surgeon's attention and we end up sitting in the exam room for three hours before even being seen. The surgeon apologizes for the hold-up, checks Wayne's eyes, then pronounces them well healed and that there is already a noticeable improvement in the moisture level of both eyes. The doctor needs to have post-surgery photos taken, so we wait another half hour for someone to do this. When the nurse finally comes into the room, we are both frustrated by the delays and length of wait time. We are running out of time to get back to the vet's office to pick Maya up. I explain our situation to the nurse and ask her to please try speeding up the rest of the process. This only seems to fluster her, making things worse by her grabbing the wrong this or that, the camera not functioning, the stool is too low, etc. I recognize this as a time to just keep my mouth shut, go with it, and hope to get out of here soon.

By the time we are done and after a 45 minute drive to the vet's office, we have a mere 15 minutes before they close for the day. Still a bit frantic, I dash in to the vet's office apologizing for cutting it so close. In the exam room, a new veterinarian explains that Maya did indeed have another abscessed tooth, this time there is no suspected catalyst. I ask the vet, if it is possible she has weak or brittle teeth. She concedes that it is possible and that given her young age, circumstances of birth and early weeks of life could certainly have an impact on her health now, as well as in the future. She advises that in this type of situation, vigilance is important and to be as proactive as possible with her health in general.

Only three months in to 2010, it has been rough so far. One crisis after another, one battle after another, it is about time we had a break. I am so desperate for some relief that toward the end of March when the weather has warmed enough to melt most of the snow, we all head to the park to get some fresh air, sunshine and exercise. Most of the snow has melted by now, leaving just a thin layer in the shaded areas. Today the sun is shining brightly, making it feel warmer than the actual upper fifties temperatures. The dogs are beyond excited to get out of the house and just run. We have the park to ourselves, so I drop their leashes and let them roam freely. They are having a ball, racing around with joyous wild abandon, exploring every nook and cranny while criss-crossing the park from one end to the other.

After walking around the whole perimeter of the park, Wayne and I sit on the steps to one of the sliding boards soaking up the sunshine while watching the dogs play. We have been at the park for an hour when we start to feel a bit chilled and decide to wrap it up. The dogs are over at the edge of the park where it is bordered by a good sized creek. When I call them to follow us toward the parking lot, Maya responds right away by trotting toward us. Zip is not quite ready to stop his explorations and continues sniffing along the bank where the geese and ducks have paths worn in the ground. Calling to him one more time, I watch as he lifts his head, takes one step toward us and then suddenly disappears, over the edge of the bank.

Screaming his name, I reach the edge of the bank in five or six running steps and fall to my knees in the snow to peer over the edge. My heart drops into my stomach as I take in the situation. He has slid over the edge onto a 4 or 5 inch ledge half way down the muddy bank. The extremely fast flowing, snowmelt swollen creek is about five feet below the edge of the bank. If he falls in, he'll be downstream and out of reach before I could even react. In the few seconds it takes me to assess the situation, Zip tries to climb up the bank only to slide back down to his ledge in the mud. I can see his eyes rolling wildly. He knows he is in trouble and is starting to panic.

I've got to keep him calm while trying to get him back up onto dry ground. Laying down flat on the snow wet ground; I carefully reach down toward him. He is about a foot out of reach. Keeping my voice calm and soothing, I try to coax him toward me,

"Come on Zip, let's get out of this mess and go home."

He stands up on his hind legs, stretching toward me, yet all I can do is touch the tip of his nose. I can't get a hold of him. He begins to whine. I stretch forward a little bit more but feel my center of balance shifting downward and have to scoot back to my original spot. The mud is thick and sticky, every move he makes causes him to sink further into the mud and already his short legs have disappeared into the muck.

I've got to think. I can't rely on Wayne's strength to hold me while I stretch down further. A quick glance around shows me, we are still the only ones in the park. I keep talking calmly to Zip... telling him soothingly "Good boy, you stay." I am afraid that if he tries further to get up on his own, he will slide, miss the ledge and end up in the water or even become further imbedded in the mire.

Maybe with a stick or piece of tree branch, I could reach his now mud caked leash and pull him up that way. Another glance around reveals, even though there were numerous branches downed by the snows, the park was either cleared of debris already or none came down here. By now, Wayne and Maya both, are watching from a few feet away,

"Son, keep a good hold on her leash. We don't need two dogs over the bank."

"Is Zip okay? Can you get him?" Wayne questions, fearfully.

"I'm trying, but he is just out of reach and scared."

An idea occurs to me. I have seen on the Animal Cops show on Animal Planet dogs and cats lifted out of similar situations with a catch pole or leash looped over the neck.

"Quick Wayne, unhook Maya's leash and toss it over here. Hold on to her, don't let her go." I instruct.

He does as told. I form a loop with the leash and try to drop it down over Zip's head, no good. He turns his head and the loop slides off to the side. Three more attempts also prove unsuccessful. Each try has caused him to turn his head and now he is chest deep in the mud and I can hear the suction pulling against him when he tries to move. I can no longer see whether he is able to move his legs anymore. It does not appear so. The only thing he is moving is his head. Frustrated, I put my head down on my arm, fighting my own panic and tears.

"Mom, somebody else is here. There are people over there on the other side of the park." Wayne's excited voice, breaks through my battle to control the rising panic I feel.

"Run baby. Go tell them I need help. Tell them our dog is stuck in the mud, over the bank. Go, quick. I need help."

As Wayne and Maya are running for help, I try one more time to loop the leash over his head. I wonder if I would be able to pull him out even if I do get the loop over his head. I don't know how strong the suction is. Amazingly, this time I do get it over his head and pulling it taut, I start to pull up. At first feeling the resistance of the unyielding mud, but then a sudden release of the pressure, allowing me to yank him up and over the edge of the bank in one second long hoist.

I fall back in relief with Zip cradled against me. We are both shaking uncontrollably. I turn around and see Wayne, Maya and the other park visitor heading toward us,

"I got him, I got him and we're okay." I call out to the advancing stranger, who then throws up a hand in acknowledgement before turning back in the other direction.

I am still sitting on the wet ground cradling Zip in my arms when Wayne and Maya make their way back to us. Maya's relief is clearly evident as she wiggles her way out of Wayne's arms to nuzzle and lick Zip's muzzle as she whines her concern. He is still shaking, almost violently now. He is covered in thick, sticky, smelly mud and does not seem to be as alert as normal. I take off my jacket, which is already mud smeared and wrap him up snuggly. I stay sitting with him in my lap and begin to rub his body vigorously. Maya has positioned herself directly in front of us, watching Zip ever so closely. A minute or so later, he begins to turn his head and look around. Still somewhat dazed, but coming to. When he looks up at me, I see his eyes are focused and his tail gives a few little wags against my leg.

I begin checking him all over and not finding any obvious injuries, set him on the ground, watching as he takes a few tentative, wobbly steps. All seems to be in working order. We stand up and begin making our way back toward the car letting Zip walk on his own hoping this will help warm him up faster and also clean off some of the mud. Reaching the car, I look back over the park and clearly see Zip's trail of cast off mud through the grass and snow. He is still trembling, but not as bad now. Still, I wrap him up in my jacket again, settle him in the back seat and turn the heat on in the car for the short trip back home. Zip is 10 years old, this episode has got to be hard on him. I can only hope, not too hard.

Back at the house, we put the muddy leashes and jackets directly into the washing machine. Zip goes straight into the sink while Wayne retrieves towels and my bath robe from upstairs and I fill up the sink with warm water for Zip to soak in until I get out of my muddy clothes and give him a good scrubbing. Wayne watches him as I change into my bath robe then drain and refill the sink with fresh warm water. I have to change the water three times before I can even begin to actually wash him. He appears to be fully alert now and I take that as a good sign, but he has not stopped trembling and is now whining under his breath. We're not out of the woods yet. It takes two good shampooing's to clean off all of the mud, which had found its way into every crease and fold of his little body.

I wrap him into a towel, lay him on the couch, put a heating pad on top of the towel and then lay a blanket over top of all that. As I sit down beside him to rub his head, Maya assumes control of the situation, wrapping her body around his head when she lies down with him. Every inch of him is now being warmed by either Maya or the heating pad and blanket. We all stay in these positions for the next hour. Zip has quit whining now and does not appear to be trembling anymore. I cannot tell for certain, the only part of him visible is a small portion of one ear. I reach up under the blanket, lay my hand on his side and feel... he is indeed breathing steadily and no longer trembling, so I turn off the heating pad but leave it in place for the residual heat.

Another hour passes. Both dogs are sleeping soundly when it is time to start supper. On a normal day, they both know this routine and join me in the kitchen for the preparations. Today, neither one stirs when I get up from the couch. Knowing sleep is probably the best thing for Zip right now, I leave them be. Just before I am ready to call Wayne downstairs to eat, I turn around and there in the doorway, both dogs are sitting expectantly with wagging tails. Well, that's a good sign.

"Hey, there old man. Are you feeling good enough to eat your supper?" I question Zip.

He stretches, does his usual snuffly sneeze and then barks once in response. Maya prances and whines expectantly, so I fill up their bowls and watch gratefully as Zip practically inhales his food and then tries to go for Maya's. I pick him up and hold him while Maya finishes her food. He feels nice and warm now. He is not trembling and gives me kisses as I inspect his nose, mouth, eyes and ears. He looks like his old self again and the next few days confirm he has no residual after affects from his scare.

CHAPTER 7

SPRING has finally arrived... the nightmare winter of 2010 is over! We are resuming our favorite outdoor activities anew; gardening, visiting parks, cooking out, and spending time with family. During a shopping trip, we run into the pet store, just because we are at the same mall and find what turns out to be an absolute must have for Zippy. It is a dog sweatshirt, boldly emblazoned on the back, "Trouble Finds Me." I have to get it. Nothing could describe Zip any better. To make sure that Maya doesn't feel left out; I also find her a pretty little yellow sundress for dogs. It is adorable and I can't wait to see them both in their new outfits.

It used to be very hard to find dog shirts that would fit my dogs. Most of them had some sort of legs attached to them and dachshund legs are far shorter than most other breeds of dogs. If the shirt fit in the body and had legs attached, the dachshund's legs would be too short, causing them to walk right out of the leg holes, getting their legs caught up inside of the shirt looking like a big stuffed sausage and unable to walk. Amusing to see, but not very practical. In the last year or so, there has been a wider selection of dog shirts available and we can now find some that do not have added legs, just holes for the dogs legs to fit through. This works much better for dachshunds and I am a bit chagrined to admit that both of my dogs each have several different shirts or in Maya's case, dresses to wear.

For Zip this is more out of comfort. He gets cold very easily and seems to be more affected by the cold weather as he is getting older. The little sweatshirts help to keep him warm. Since Maya has longer hair, she does not get cold nearly as easily and her dresses are purely fashionable. I don't dress them up frequently. When I do they are both eager to put on their outfits, independently sticking their heads through the opening when held open for them and prancing about, looking oh so pleased with themselves.

I readily admit that since I only had one child and that being a boy, I never had the opportunity to dress a little girl in pretty, frilly dresses and that I am now getting to experience that with Maya and her dresses. It really is enjoyable to pick out dresses for her. They are so adorable and look almost exactly like a little girl's dress. I swear she knows how cute she is with a dress on; she struts along like she is the princess willing everyone to admire her.

My sister and the kids are making their annual Easter visit and this year shows Maya's level of tolerance to be much improved. She actually plays with the kids, albeit just in brief episodes. This is huge progress from last year's visit. Five years old now, her maturity is definitely showing.

During their visit, the kids ask to go to their favorite park here, which turns out to be the same one where Zip had his episode over the river bank. I agree we can go there, but explain what happened to Zip and that they must make sure when playing or walking him to stay far away from the river bank. I am actually hoping he will remember his fright and stay away on his own. At the park, it soon becomes evident he did not learn his lesson and from our first steps into the park, starts pulling against the leash to go right over to where he fell down the bank. I spend the rest of our time at the park keeping Zip on leash and with me on the other side of the park. He is given no opportunity to have a repeat accident.

I always try to have some activity planned for the kids to partake in when they are here, this visit is no exception. Wayne and I have decided we will have a competition based on one of the games from his current favorite TV show, Minute To Win It.

The game is to pull all of the tissues out of a box using only one hand in under 60 seconds and eight boxes later, there is a mountain of tissues on the dining room table and floor, proving to be irresistible for the dogs. They burrow under the pile, pop their heads up through the drift and then pounce at each other, scattering tissues everywhere. The kids then start throwing piles of tissues up into the air, as they drift down, the dogs' snatch them out of the air then toss them aside, only to grab for another. By the time we are all done, we have quite a mess, but have had fun and a lot of laughs, not to mention the "Bag 'O Tissues" I gather back up to be used as intended, rather than wasted.

A mere two and a half weeks after Easter and Maya suddenly shows a dramatic decrease in her typical activity level. At first there are no other symptoms but later that evening, the simple act of hopping off the couch, elicits a cry of pain. My guard goes up. I lift her up and down from the couch for the rest of the evening and also carry her up the stairs at bedtime. The next morning, she appears to be fine, until she starts to follow me upstairs to get ready for work. About halfway up, she screams in pain, freezing on the spot. Running down to where she is... I gently pick her up, another scream of pain. Oh geez, this does not sound good. Setting her down on the floor, I watch as she freezes in place, does not move at all. Zip has followed us upstairs and if I was not already concerned, his behavior would have done it. He gives her one cautious lick to the muzzle and then lies down beside her, whining softly under his breath. I am fully aware that dachshund's are apt to have ruptured disc's in their backs and that any suspected issue needs to be checked out immediately. I call the vet, tell them I'm on the way and Maya's symptoms, then call work and adjust my client schedule.

On the way to the vet's office, Maya lies in the front seat not moving, in the waiting room, she lies on the bench not moving, in the exam room she lies on the table not moving. I carry her from place to place and each time I gently pick her up, she screams. I am really getting scared by the time the vet tech comes to take her back to be examined. Ten agonizing minutes later, the new vet comes in with Maya in her arms.

She begins to explain, there is a slight swelling around one of the discs in Maya's back. It is not ruptured, only a slight inflammation surrounding the disc and can be treated. I breathe a thankful sigh of relief and then listen carefully to the instructions for her care. She is prescribed Prednisolone over the next ten days in decreasing dosages, ordered decreased activity, no jumping, climbing stairs, or strenuous activities. Normally, I would think this to be an impossible task with Maya but by the way she is acting today, it won't be much of a problem.

The trip back home is identical to the one in to the vet's office, only now I am not as concerned and thinking how to keep her calm while I go to work. Wayne will be home but, I'm not sure how observant he will be about preventing her from being over active. I decide putting her in the training crate for the few hours is probably the best option. Back at the house, I explain her injury to Wayne. Then I bring the crate down from the attic and line it with a soft pillow. Finally, after carrying her down and then back up the three steps to the backyard, I settle her into the crate until my short work day is done.

Wayne reports Maya did very well in the crate while I was gone. She never whined or tried to get out, she just slept. The rest of the evening, more of the same, she lies calmly, dozing on and off. Over the remaining days on her medication she shows small improvements. She becomes very cautious in her activities, at first just accepting my carrying her up and down the stairs, lifting her on and off the couch, but then expecting it, actually waiting for me to pick her up.

The last couple of days, the medication is given only every other day. I notice a decrease in Maya's activity again. By the time she has taken the last half of a pill, and gone two days without a pill, she begins screaming in apparent pain once more. I call the vet's office; explain the situation, this time asking to have

Dr. Kendrick see her, only to be told he is no longer actively seeing patients. The receptionist informs me there is another new vet available if I am not comfortable with the one who saw Maya last time.

"No, no, it's not that. I just trust Dr. Kendrick more since we have dealt with only him for so many years. I'll see the same doctor we had before, if Dr. Kendrick trusts her enough to take over his patients, I should too."

Back in the exam room again, the new doctor reports the inflammation has gone down dramatically and that Maya should not be experiencing any pain at this point, but since she obviously is we'll put her on another, but shorter round of the medication and add a muscle relaxer as well.

She does better on this round of medication and is almost back to her normal self, except for still being carried up and down the inside steps and lifted on and off the couch. Pop Pop came over a few days ago and using a wide barn board, made a ramp over the three steps from the back porch to the yard so Maya can navigate that area easily on her own. She seems to take great enjoyment in this. She apparently remembers the obstacles from agility class and knew immediately how to use it. The ramp is still there today.

The end of this second round of medication brings the exact same result. Within a couple of days, Maya is back to screaming in pain. Sometimes it is when we pick her up, but other times it is for no apparent reason at all. She will be lying down and just start yelping out of the blue. Back to the vet's office we go again. The exam this time shows the inflammation is completely gone. There is no physical reason for her behavior. Suddenly remembering the incident years ago, when Maya's paw had been accidentally stepped on, I ask the vet,

"Could this be a sympathy behavior?"

"Actually at this point, yes it could be." she responds.

"She did this before, a few years ago. I was sure fooled then and I guess I've been fooled again."

"Well, she did start with a slight injury this time. She just carried it a little too far. Your little girl is pretty good at it, very convincing."

"Okay, so how do I get her past this?" I question finally.

Thinking for a moment, the vet then suggests that I try now to encourage a slow increase in activity. Prove to her that she is fine now and can go back to her normal self.

I start by trying to take her on short walks by herself. Just up and down the street in front of the house. She does not give up her ruse. She walks down the street ever so slowly and carefully, but on her own four paws. Once we turn around and head back up, the barely noticeable incline to our house, she sits down, refusing to walk on her own. I pick her up and carry her the rest of the way home. The second attempt on the next day... exact same response, but this time I do not pick her up. I drop the leash and start walking away. She sits there in the middle of the street watching me for a few steps then lo and behold; she begins to follow after me. Slowly, she continues to follow me. Somewhat reluctantly, all the way back to the house which is a distance of no more than twenty feet.

We do this every day for the next week. Each day she makes it a few steps further before sitting down in her attempt at sympathy inducing protest. I do not give in and am finally able to walk her down the street and all the way back up without her stopping. This is still far below her normal activity but, is progress and I'll take it.

I begin expanding our walks to around the immediate area. Trying to take a different route each time and finally feel she is ready to walk the maybe three block distance down town to the post office and town hall. She just got another new dress and I decide to dress her up for the occasion, hoping the show off in her will help overcome any protesting she may have planned. I take Zip along this time and the walk down the mild hill is of no concern. She even stops to let a few neighbors admire her dress, before prancing on to the next admirer.

We complete our tasks and visiting and head back up the hill toward the house. Maya begins to slow down almost immediately upon meeting the incline. Thinking maybe her dress is hindering her now or making her too hot... I stop, remove the dress and stick it into my back pocket. The three of us walk another ten feet or so, Maya is now lagging so far behind that she is at the full length of her leash, behind me. Zip meanwhile is at the full length of his leash, ahead of me, not used to this slow pace. I am walking sideways, seemingly being pulled apart by two dogs at different speeds. This feels just like when Maya was a puppy and first learning to walk on a leash. Zip and I stop, waiting for her to catch up. She just plods along, head down, ears dragging the ground, looking like she is completely spent. Fearing I may be pushing her too far, I pick her up and begin back up the hill, carrying her in my arms.

It does not take long in this manner, before I am winded and struggling to manage both dogs. As I stop at an intersection to cross the street, our neighbor is coming up behind us in his truck. Turning around, I wave him down, panting for breath, I ask him,

"Jon, could you take Maya back to the house with you, for me?"

"Is her back still hurting her?"

"She is getting better, but I think I may have pushed a little further today than she was ready for. If you could take her back to the house and put her in the back yard, Zip and I will be there in a few minutes. I just can't carry her up the hill and hold on to him as well." I respond.

One of Jon's buddies is with him; he jumps into the back of the truck... I place Maya in his arms and then start to hand him her dress, which is still in my back pocket,

"Oh no," he says, shaking his head. "I'll hold the dog, but I'm not holding some frilly pink dog dress too!"

I tuck the dress back into my pocket, telling Maya to stay and then Zip and I start to trudge up the rest of the hill. Almost at the top, one of the neighbors to previously admire Maya in her dress on our way down the hill, sees only me and Zip walking up the hill with no Maya and her dress hanging out of my back pocket.

Alarmed, she calls out, "Where is Maya, did something happen?"

Embarrassed, I relate that Maya hitched a ride with Jon. The walk was too much, too soon, as far as her back was concerned.

"You mean, he gave Maya a ride but left you and Zip to finish the hill, anyway?"

"Yep, but I just asked him to take Maya. Zip and I are fine. We're still in good enough shape to finish our walk, we're almost home anyway."

Back at home there is Maya, waiting patiently by the back door for Zip and I to return. The rest of that evening and the next several days show no after affects from our attempted walk down town, but neither does she revert back to her normal self again.

We start going to as many different places in our immediate area for walks as often as possible. Hoping that at some point, her natural curiosity and happy go lucky attitude will over-ride her caution or manipulation game, which ever this is. I have to give it to her; she does not let it go easily. By now, a full month has gone by since the initial incident and she still mopes around at home and out in the community. I have her on an herbal regime to improve muscle, joint and nerve function and strength, as well as using massage for circulation and muscle soreness. She refuses to even attempt navigating stairs and in all honesty, I do not push this issue. We continue to carry her up and down the inside stairs. She will now, jump onto the couch by herself, but will not jump down. The same goes for the car; she will jump into it, but not out.

We have been invited to a picnic get together over Memorial Day weekend. This will be an all day trip and we will be taking both dogs along. Zippy has been there before and knows these people well. Maya however, does not. This will be a whole new experience for her. I am hopeful she will be so overwhelmed with new stimulus that she just forgets about her back. On the other hand, I am concerned that it will be too much for her and she really does injure herself again. We'll just have to watch her very carefully and adjust to her needs.

The long drive ends without a hitch and we arrive at our destination about an hour before lunch. Both dogs are eager to get out of the car and see what new adventure is in store for them today. Zip is out the car heading straight for the action in the midst of the dozen people gathered in the yard for the picnic. I carry Maya from the car, up to the fenced in yard, before setting her down to explore on her own. As I watch her carefully at first, someone tells me not to worry about her, the yard is completely fenced in and safe. I explain about her recent injury and her apparent self-imposed lengthy recovery.

There is so much for them to explore, as well as three other small dogs and some outside cats to play with. I keep an eye on Maya, but otherwise, let her do her own thing. She starts out being cautious and slow moving. Eventually the temptations get the better of her and soon she is trotting here, there and everywhere with no apparent concern for her back. While we are sitting down to eat, all of the dogs realize there are kids with food and come running to find the best spot to sit and wait for something to fall. Even Maya, and yes, she is running across the yard with the other dogs. I can't help but shake my head and smile while pointing her out... short little legs a blur in the grass, ears flouncing up and down with each stride. Finally, I sigh, mission accomplished. She has forgotten to play the role she has clung to for the last month, what a relief.

The day turns out to be rather hot for this time of year and the dogs decide that under the canopy is the coolest place to be. Soon, there is a dog stretched out, under every other chair. Except that is, for Zippy, he only spends a few minutes at a time under the canopy. The cats are far too compelling for him. He repeatedly races around after the cats for about ten minutes, comes dragging over to the canopy, gets a drink of water, then flops down under a chair, panting heavily for another ten minutes just to jump up and do it all over again. Maya watches each of his forays but, now shows no interest in following him. Her long hair makes her less tolerant of the heat and she is quite content to sit in my lap acting like the princess she is convinced she is.

Our visit has drawn to an end and both dogs seem to be more than ready to load into the air-conditioned car for the trip home. Turns out, they were both so exhausted, they sleep all the way home. The next few days prove that Maya has indeed, realized her back no longer hurts and that she can get back to enjoying all of the things she normally does. Things have returned to normal except for one thing, the stairs. Maya continues to use the ramp placed over the porch steps and absolutely refuses to even attempt the stairs inside the house. It appears that she remembers the stairs as the source of her most severe pain. She will use steps at locations other than our house, so I know she can do it. I want her to realize on her own, the stairs are manageable again. I start by not carrying her up each time I go upstairs. The first few times, she sits at the bottom, whining, until I come back downstairs. Then for a few more days, she hesitantly, climbs the three steps to the landing where she sits and whines, until I come back down.

Eventually, she does make her way all the way up the stairs on her own accord and seems to be quite pleased with herself. Three months after her initial injury, she has made her way back to full recovery and is now able to go up and down the stairs easily, on her own.

August is usually a busy month for us. This year is shaping up to follow the same pattern. The month begins with the local fair and a major MDA fund-raiser, both on the same day. The fair actually runs for an entire week, ending on the same Saturday as the Poker Run that donates half of their proceeds to MDA on Wayne's behalf. One of the events on the final day of the fair is the pet show. Zippy and Maya will both participate. This is a just for fun competition, with categories such as longest & shortest hair, longest & shortest ears, longest dog, prettiest costume and so on.

Each dog is to be entered in 3 different categories. I enter each of my dogs into the categories that apply best to them individually. The competition begins at 10 a.m. Both dogs know something fun is about to happen, they are curious and eager to begin. The start of each category begins with the entered dogs being called onto the stage to be judged. Maya happens to be the first of our two called up. Wayne holds on to Zip while Maya and I climb up onto the stage for her to be judged. She does wonderful, is tolerant and friendly with the judges as well as all the other dogs and people on the crowded stage.

Zip watches our every move, patiently from Wayne's lap and then greets Maya enthusiastically when we return to our seats. Maya is, typically full of herself and almost appears to be asking Zip,

"Did ya see me?"

When he is called up onto the stage, she is not so patient, whining and wiggling in Wayne's lap, wanting to be the center of attention. Zip also does extremely well. He is Mister Rock Solid, always calm and sedate, taking everything in stride, without batting an eye. He stands still for his measurements and then merely gazes around until the judging is done. By the third category, I realize there is another dog there named Maya. I watch in amusement, as my Maya hears the other dog's name called and starts toward the stage on her own, thinking it is her turn again. I do have a hold of her leash. Otherwise, she would have trotted right up there for every category, just as confident as can be.

The last category for Zip is for laziest dog. Before knowing the actual details of the competition, I had a little obedience routine planned for both dogs to perform and had brought along Zip's dog bed and blanket as props. After realizing the categories, I scratched that idea, but thought it would encourage

Zip to show off his lazy side. As soon as Zip and I mounted the stage, I set down his bed, laid the blanket over it and commanded him to "go to bed." Just like at home, he used his nose to lift up the side of the blanket then crawled under the blanket and into the bed, sitting down with the blanket draped over his body leaving just his head out to peer around at the crowd in bemusement.

Needless to say, Zip took the blue ribbon for "Laziest Dog." Not to be outdone, Maya's final category is the one most suited to her personality, "Prettiest Costume." I put on her little yellow sundress, fasten a yellow bow on each ear and watch her prance up onto the stage to be admired. What a ham. She preens and poses for the judges and as if on command, even bats her eyes when the judges stop in front of her. When she is presented with the third place ribbon, she is just as proud as if it were the first place.

The judges then announce there will be two additional categories previously unannounced, one for "Reserve Champion" and one for "Prettiest Pet." For the "Reserve Champion," all the dogs who won a ribbon in the other categories are called onto the stage and after an obviously pre-planned, dramatic conference by the judges; all the dogs are given blue ribbons. For the "Prettiest Pet," the judges call specific dogs back onto the stage, including our Maya. After another dramatic conference, the judges announce they are unable to choose just one dog as prettiest and award blue ribbons to all on stage. Maya actually jumps up and down in joy, when she is given her ribbon. Does she really know? I don't put anything past her; I think she has figured it out.

By the time the pet show is over, it is noon and the fairgrounds are filling up. The food vendors are going full steam, the sights and smells have got to be sensory overload for the dogs, but they each have their ribbons attached to their collars, three for Zip and four for Maya. They seem intent on parading to the exit in full regalia while Wayne and I struggle to manage Zip's bed and blanket, Maya's dress and the seven small bags of dog food, given as prizes. The temperature has risen significantly over the last two hours and even though we are parked fairly close to the exit, the dog's ribbons are dragging the ground when we make it to the car. A good nap in the air conditioned house is next on the day's agenda, before Wayne and I head down for the Poker Run's After Party.

Many of the rider's participate in this run because of Wayne and since we have been doing this for several years now, they have watched him grow and always ask about his health. It makes for a very long day, but neither of us would ever think of missing it.

Later this month we have plans to visit with Bonnie and Roger at their farm for a day. We haven't been there for a while and we are all looking forward to it. The long car ride clues the dogs in that this is a special outing. Each time I stop the car, they are ready to explode out the back door and begin the adventure. When we stop at our final destination, they react in the same manner. This time able to actually exit the car off leash and discover where we are. It does not take long at all for both of them to realize we are on the farm. We exchange hugs with Bonnie and Roger, the dogs exchange sniffs with Oscar and Shelly, then all four dogs take off to explore.

Zip apparently, is the leader at first. Maya follows Zip. Oscar follows Maya and Shelly follows Oscar. It is a veritable dog train. Shelly is the first to give up, returning to the picnic table briefly and then positioning herself beside Bonnie on the covered swing. Maya is the next to cease the exploration, returning to relax under the picnic table. Sadly for her, Oscar is apparently enamored with her and follows her every move, trying to get her to at least acknowledge him, if not actively play. She is, so not interested. Flat out ignores him, giving him the coldest shoulder I have ever seen. Oscar is sent inside to cool off and give Maya a break. Zip has finally completed his mission of exploring every nook and cranny on his agenda and returns to join Maya under the picnic table.

While we are all relaxing and catching up, Roger's mom walks over from her house, next door, with her little dog Chico. He is a friendly, laid back terrier and Maya takes to him immediately. She really feels comfortable with his energy and surprisingly begins to pounce at him, initiating a good romping play that entices Zip and Shelly to join in. This is the only place where we can absolutely leave the dogs off leash and feel confident they are safe and will not stray off the property. They relish the opportunity and freedom, to just be dogs, doing what dogs like to do.

During one of their play breaks, I notice that Maya has the start of a hot spot on her back. She has not been licking or scratching at it, but there it is. I realize, that is probably what got Oscar worked up. I did not bring her spray along, so there is not much I can do about it for now. It does not seem to be bothering her; I'll make sure to treat it as soon as we get home.

The time to head for home has arrived. Sadly, we say our goodbyes and then load into the car. It is another quiet trip. Everybody else, in the car sleeps for the entire time, only waking when we return to our town. We had a very relaxing visit, allowing me to recharge my batteries before starting a new job in a couple of days. The schedule of this new job is going to be a big change for all of us. Wayne will have to show more independence for himself and take on more of the dogs care. I spend the next day's preparing him for the new tasks ahead of him, hoping he can rise to the occasion. The next few weeks, prove that he indeed can. There have been a few bumps to iron out, but we have all adjusted to the changes.

The holidays are over and winter is upon us once again. Hopefully we will have an easier one than last year. Zippy is 11 years old now and it shows. All of his markings that were tan have turned completely white and the black areas are becoming peppered with white hairs. He has zero tolerance for cold, wet or snowy weather, going out to do his business right at the bottom of the porch steps then barking impatiently to be let back in, within a mere few minutes.

This year for Christmas, we got him a "Snuggie" dog bed that he absolutely loves. It is like two fleece blankets sewn together, forming a pocket for the dog to curl up in. He is displaying some stiffness in his joints now and I thought this would be comfortable for him. I guess it is, when he does crawl out of it, he is as toasty warm as a heating pad. Through all the now visible signs of aging, his physique remains muscular and trim. He is still a good looking dog.

Maya is now 6 years old. She has mellowed out

some, but remains a happy go lucky, fun loving dog, full of curiosity and sass. She has become in tune to when her humans do not feel well. If one of us is sick in bed, she will beg to be lifted up and then cuddle up under the blankets and against the chest where she will remain until the bed bound person stirs or gets up. At no other time will she stay under blankets for more than a few minutes. She is the absolute best bed buddy when you are sick.

Her Christmas present this year was a dog mind puzzle, a plastic tray with holes for treats to be hidden in then covered by either plastic cups or a sliding lid. It took her no time at all to figure out how to get to the treats. She is just way too smart for her own good.

We have significant snow on the ground right now. Maya has outgrown romping through the snow, she does not venture any further than Zippy does when let out to potty and no longer pulls the snowballs off her fur. Now she just waits for them to melt on their own. During the winter she is content to get her exercise indoors; fetching one of her fuzzy tail tennis balls or playing "keep away" with her pink soccer ball. Her health is good right now, even though it is an almost constant battle to stay on top of her skin allergies. Her back is completely healed and as of today, her teeth are not posing any problems. Not a single day goes by without either Wayne or I telling her she is beautiful.

Both of these dogs bring so much joy into our lives, as well as each other's. They are my "Pair of Puppies." I can't help but wonder how their futures will unfold in the coming years; one will surely pass before the other. Will the remaining one be able to go on afterward? Maybe, I should not think so far ahead or worry about the inevitable. Regardless, we continue to love and enjoy each day with this pair, who both had less than desirable beginnings in their lives. I believe that we have given them ten times more than what they lacked before coming to us.

Zippy's early days will apparently, remain a mystery that I can only guess about. Maya's early days are crystal clear in their neglectful cruelty. There is sometimes a sense of regret over inadvertently falling prey to the puppy mill ruse not once, but twice; both so artfully concealed, vehemently denied, and unfortunately, only small examples of a huge nationwide embarrassment. The damage done to these dogs is sometimes easily evident, yet other times may not be present as problems for several years or more. The heartache felt by the families who bring these dogs into their lives to love and cherish is another form of cruelty in itself that I am sure the operators of these facilities, either never think about or do not care enough to think about.

I would not trade a single moment I have had with these two. Through all the challenges and obstacles they have faced, we overcame them together... with love, compassion, and dedication. I would take away the callousness they were born into, but I can't. I can be aware in the future to be hyper-vigilant in researching the circumstances of any new pet's arrival to this world.

Many states either have or are debating legislation to ban "puppy mill" type facilities. Our state has this on their agenda for the coming legislative session and after living through Maya's experiences with her, I truly hope it is passed and yet, know in my heart it will not be the end-all for these practices.

Maya's tale, in reality, is far from over. She has many more adventures ahead of her and I look forward to sharing them all with her. Maya's tale, for the purpose of this book, is complete. I have spoken for her, to bring awareness to the lifelong consequences of being born into a "puppy mill" and to raise the awareness of potential pet owners. Ultimately, the only way this practice will end, is if it stops being profitable. The people who participate in the "puppy mill" practice know we will not endorse the true nature of their facilities and know how to mislead, deceive and cover up what we do not want to see. We the consumer, have the power to investigate where our pets are coming from. Reputable breeders will welcome questions, animal shelters and rescue groups are both overwhelmed trying to save animals in bad situations and find them permanent loving homes. Maya's tale ends as a happy one. There are many others who deserve the same.

Ω

January 12, 2011

Where to Find this Book

For a limited time only, *Maya's Tale* is available exclusively from the Web sites of the author, the publisher and its printer(s)

http://www.unlimitedpublishing.com/moyer

Order by mail: Unlimited Publishing LLC, Box 99, Nashville, IN 47448

Also for Dog Lovers

Redstripe and Other Dachshund Tales

The cult classic series by the late Jack Magestro

http://www.unlimitedpublishing.com/magestro

Anything But a Dog!

http://www.unlimitedpublishing.com/saunders

How Can You Give Up That Adorable Puppy?

Stories of Guide Dogs Growing Up

http://www.unlimitedpublishing.com/rebmann

About the Book

This story is based on real life. The author acquired not one, but two dachshund puppies — both ultimately found to have been bred under less than desirable circumstances. Zippy, the first dachshund, was purchased from a popular chain pet store, just months before a nationwide investigation into dog breeding. Five years later, having been educated on the pet store practices, the author sought to find a responsible breeder for a second dachshund to join her family. The heartbreaking reality of Maya's breeding becomes horrifyingly evident when she is 4 years old.

About the Author

Yvonne Haldeman Moyer was born in Pennsylvania, grew up around military bases, married and divorced, raising a son with Muscular Dystrophy alone for the past 18 years, she has been active in many different endeavors, enjoying challenging outlets for her inherent creativity. Since taking residence in West Virginia, she has been employed in a variety of different capacities, from in home care aide, to small town elected official, as well as Director of a non-profit organization, and currently at the local university. Her now adult son and two dachshunds keep her 1918 Victorian home full of joy and vitality.

Made in the USA
Charleston, SC
07 April 2012